How
to
Enjoy
Writing

A BOOK OF AID AND COMFORT

D1111779

Collaborations by Janet and Isaac Asimov

LAUGHING SPACE
NORBY, THE MIXED-UP ROBOT
NORBY'S OTHER SECRET
NORBY AND THE LOST PRINCESS
NORBY AND THE INVADERS
NORBY AND THE QUEEN'S NECKLACE

How to Enjoy Writing

A BOOK OF AID AND COMFORT

by

Janet and Isaac Asimov

Cartoons by Sidney Harris

Walker and Company
720 Fifth Avenue
New York, N.Y. 10019

The publisher is grateful to the following for permission to reprint from copy-righted material:

Isaac Asimov, © 1980 (Page 60)
Davis Publications, Inc., © 1978 (Page 8), 1979 (page 61), 1980 (page 20), 1981 (page 63), 1986 (page 125)
Mercury Press, Inc., © 1972 (page 84)
The New Leader, Inc., © 1962 (page 16)
Nightfall, Inc., © 1982 (page 129)
Bill Pronzini, Charles G. Waugh, Martin Greenberg, © 1985 (page 80)
The Writer, © 1979 (page 38)
Writer's Digest, © 1986 (page 100)

First published in the United States of America in 1987 by the Walker Publishing Company, Inc.

Published simultaneously in Canada by Thomas Allen & Son Canada, Limited, Markham, Ontario.

Library of Congress Cataloging-in-Publication Data
Asimov, Janet.
    How to enjoy writing.

    Bibliography: p.
    1. Authorship.   I. Asimov, Isaac, 1920–
II. Title.
PN147.A723   1987   808'.02   86-26785
ISBN 0-8027-0945-1
ISBN 0-8027-7303-6 (pbk.)

Printed in the United States of America

10 9 8 7 6 5

Book design by Laurie McBarnette

TO THE VERSATILE ENGLISH LANGUAGE—THE BEST TOOL
A WRITER EVER HAD.

Contents

How to Enjoy Writing

A BOOK OF AID AND COMFORT

Introduction

Human beings live longer and better when they enjoy what they do. We hope this book will increase the enjoyment of writing for you who are working writers, or wish to be.

You will no doubt discover that you share with us certain assumptions:

1. Anything is more fun when you improve your skills.
2. You already know a lot about writing and writers.
3. Coping with the life of a writer isn't so difficult.
4. The effort of writing is part of the fun.
5. Writing is a GREAT occupation.

As we approach an experience that should be fun, we should remain open to its possibilities. We should not let ourselves be adversely influenced by what others say or by what we say to ourselves about it.

—STEWART W. HOLMES

The test of a vocation is the love of the drudgery it involves.

—LOGAN PEARSALL SMITH

Let each day's work absorb your entire energies, and satisfy your widest ambition.

—WILLIAM OSLER

I have never understood why "hard work" is supposed to be pitiable. True, some work is soul-destroying when it is done against the grain, but when it is part of a "making"

1

how can you grudge it? You get tired, of course, often in despair, but the struggle, the challenge, the feeling of being extended as you never thought you could be is fulfilling and deeply, deeply satisfying.

—RUMER GODDEN

Well, I wouldn't say I was in the "great" class, but I had a great time while I was trying to be great.

—HARRY S. TRUMAN

And perhaps old Harry has the real insight. How many of us, even the "successful" among us, are going to be *great* writers? Very few, certainly, and probably very, very few—but nothing is going to stop *any* of us from having fun while we chase that will-o-the-wisp, and having fun is what counts.

Just keep muttering to yourself: writing is a GREAT occupation, and I ENJOY WRITING!

Janet and Isaac Asimov
New York City
November 1986

P.S. Our editor pointed out that "aid and comfort" in our subtitle is used when people are accused of helping the enemy.

We laughed, but on second thought, it's true. After all, you who read this book aim at being our competitors, don't you?

—J. and I.A.

1.

The Fun Of It

Don't believe everything you've read and heard about the horrors of creative effort, but don't expect many writers to tell the truth—that they love to write. There's always the popular suspicion that if you're not actively suffering, you aren't really working and probably aren't creating anything worthwhile.

Any activity is enjoyable if:

1. You do it well.
2. You think it's worth doing.
3. You feel good while doing it (physically, emotionally, and mentally).
4. It helps others (this includes entertaining them).
5. It makes money.
6. It brings you positive response.

Launching yourself into a life of creative work does not guarantee the fulfillment of all these items immediately or ever, but you are bound to achieve one or two, and— ask any creative worker—that makes it worthwhile.

Animals seem to enjoy whatever activity they were built to do, and human beings are no exception. Humans seem particularly designed for creative work. They have large brains, the capacity for language, extraordinary hands, and good vision. We believe that all basically constructive work

3

is creative—a cook or gardener creating beauty and nourishment, a sanitation worker creating order and cleanliness in society, a medical worker helping people's bodies create healing—the list is long.

Destructive work is never creative, especially when it involves learning how to be an efficient killer with a gun or with a finger on the nuclear button.

So don't be destructive. It isn't fun, and you'll give up your human birthright of creativity.

And if you genuinely want to be or stay, a writer, consider the premise that writing is the most creative work of all, and—because it exercises the innate human ability to imagine and to communicate—the most pleasurable.

We may be slightly prejudiced about this.

2.

The Work

As a writer, you use tools that are almost all inside your head—insight, humor, knowledge, and wisdom. None of them is much use without the basic tool of language.

WORDS HAVE POWER! When you think about it, you realize that language is the most powerful tool ever invented anywhere by anyone.

> I was walking along Park Avenue and passed a blind man with a cup. I put a quarter in it, as I always do, and walked on and then words went through my head—"dark, dark, dark, amid the blaze of noon"—and then I looked at my watch and it was exactly noon and I couldn't help it; right in the middle of the street I began to cry.
> —ISAAC ASIMOV (unpublished letter)

Certain word arrangements—like Milton's "dark, dark . . . " from "Samson Agonistes")—seem to have immortality, but even if your words don't last forever, they still have power. They may entertain, help, and teach. Remember that human beings don't grow up human by themselves; they have to be taught to be human by associating with people who *communicate* with them.

Keep learning to use words with insight, humor, knowledge, and wisdom—until you fall over with quill pen in hand or nose down in the keyboard of your word processor.

LANGUAGE, THE BASIC TOOL:

Asimov's Main Rule about writing is: EITHER IT SOUNDS RIGHT OR IT DOESN'T SOUND RIGHT.

How do you know? You've spent a lifetime reading.

We interviewed a large assortment of working writers and every one of them was and still is an avid reader. Busy writers often can't read as much as they'd like to, but all of them do read for relaxation and to keep learning.

The writers generally agree that they learned to read early as children, often by being read aloud to. They say that when they are hard at work on their own writing, they can't read writers whose subjects are similar to their own, yet other writers' books stimulate their creative juices because "their stuff goes into the grooves of my mind almost as well as my own writing." Even when they find they don't like something they read, they—as writers— can learn from it.

Read on, with your eyes and mind wide open (especially when reading your own stuff!), because WORDS HAVE POWER.

I was . . . writing to a friend about the awful process of revision, and the word fell at the very end of the line. I had to hyphenate it. The word became RE-VISION. To see again. To look again. To envision again. In that instant of revelation, the kind one has on reading a familiar poem when the succession of ordinary words suddenly becomes unfamiliar, taking on a new and revelatory meaning, I knew. I was not

"WHAT DID I INVENT? MY INVENTION IS EVEN MORE REMARKABLE THAN YOURS. IT IS THE SIMPLE DECLARATIVE SENTENCE."

simply rewriting. I was being handed a second chance to dream.

—JANE YOLEN

Some people read works like the Bible and Shakespeare's plays over and over. Each time, they create new meanings from the light waves coming from the same type. In the months or years between readings they have had many experiences . . . The words do not change. The meanings, we could say, are not in the words but in the minds of the readers.

—STEWART W. HOLMES

[From I. A.'s essay *"Hints"*] First, you have to learn to use your tools, just as a surgeon has to learn to use his.

The basic tool for any writer is the English language, which means you must develop a good vocabulary and brush up on such prosaic things as spelling and grammar.

There can be little argument about vocabulary, but it may occur to you that spelling and grammar are just frills. After all, if you write great and gorgeous stories, surely the editor will be delighted to correct your spelling and grammar.

Not so! He (or she) won't be.

Besides, take it from an old warhorse, if your spelling and grammar are rotten, you won't be writing a great and gorgeous story. Someone who can't use a saw and hammer doesn't turn out stately furniture.

Even if you've been diligent at school, have developed a vocabulary, can spell "sacrilege" and "supersede" and never say "between you and I" or "I ain't never done nothing," that's still not enough. There's the subtle structure of the English sentence and the artful construction of the English paragraph. There is the clever interweaving of plot, the handling of dialogue, and a thousand other intricacies.

How do you learn that? Do you read books on how to write, or attend classes on writing, or go to writers' conferences? These are all of inspirational value, I'm sure, but they won't teach you what you really want to know.

What *will* teach you is the careful reading of the masters of English prose. This does not mean condemning yourself to years of falling asleep over dull classics. Good writers are invariably fascinating writers—the two must go together. In my opinion, the writers of English who most clearly use the correct word every time and who most artfully and deftly put together their sentences and paragraphs are Charles Dickens, Mark Twain, and P. G. Wodehouse.

Read them and others, but with attention. They represent your schoolroom. Observe what they do and try to figure out why they do it. It's no use having other people explain it to you. Until you see it for yourself and it becomes part of you, nothing will help.

But suppose that no matter how you try, you can't seem to absorb the lesson—well, it may be that you're not a writer. It's no disgrace. You can always go on to take up some slightly inferior profession like surgery or the presidency of the United States. It won't be as good, of course, but we can't all scale the heights.

USING LANGUAGE:

BE SIMPLE AND CLEAR. At least to start with. If you know how to marshal your thoughts and put them into words people can understand, you'll soon be able to express your unique self in whatever style becomes natural for you.

THINK IT THROUGH FIRST. Especially if you want to be a prolific writer. Some lucky writers manage to think so efficiently that first drafts are practically final copy. Other writers have to write almost unconsciously, waiting to see what shows up on the paper or the screen before they know what was in their heads.

HAVE FAITH IN YOUR MIND. It does a lot of work on its own time. After heavy research and deep thinking and talking to yourself (and perhaps many written drafts), set your mind free to work on the whole thing while you are doing something else, like listening to Beethoven or formatting disks (or both). Soon your mind will come up with a creative idea or a reasonable integration of data. This can be inconvenient if it happens in the middle of a conversation, or while you're standing in line at the supermarket, or just as you've started to wash your hair. If not blessed with a superb memory, mutter quietly to yourself to keep whatever it is in your cerebral cortex until you can get to the machine you use for preserving words.

Your mind may also come up with the conviction that you should start over. Okay, but never throw first efforts away too soon. They should be available to be cannibalized in the future when your mind suddenly thinks of something useful to do with them.

[Isaac in conversation] "I guess I have faith in my mind. I look inside my head and see the whole story written out, a little at a time. Part of my mind is doing all the scut work and the conscious part of me is watching in amazement, trying to channel it through my fingers into written words. When I have a lot of work to do, on many projects, part of my mind is working away on one project while I'm doing another, and I check on it now and then but it doesn't interfere with what I'm typing."

"IT'S NO USE. LISTEN TO THIS: 'LOLA WENT UP THE STEPS. THEN SHE STOPPED. THEN SHE TURNED AROUND. THEN SHE DECIDED TO GO DOWN THE STEPS...'"

TRUST THE UNIVERSE. Everything is grist for the writing mill. Even if the universe doesn't last forever, it will last longer than you, long enough for many of your words to live after you. Nothing good is really wasted.

Every human being is interesting in some way. Every life is a story, with a beginning, middle, and an end.

Everything is deep and meaningful if you look hard enough. If you don't believe this, try Zen.

LOVE AND RESPECT YOUR LANGUAGE. We love English, but then it's the only language we can write. English is the best example of a language that has simplified its grammar, losing inflection and gender compared to other languages. At the same time, English has gained an enormous vocabulary by absorbing words from all other languages.

Bad writing is often not a matter of lack of knowledge of grammar but a matter of having a tin ear for one's own language. English has the richest heritage of any language in the world, and has picked up something more than words and grammar. It has picked up a music of its own, a swinging of rhythmic syllables. Get the music right and grammar will automatically be correct and word order proper and thought clear.

Unfortunately, if you are deaf to the music of your language, then no amount of formal education and proficiency will produce more than, at best, technically accurate sentences, and at worst an illiterate jargon.

[From an unpublished letter of Isaac's] So many people find it difficult to write. They must think out the grammar and it becomes wearisome to do so. They therefore take the easy way of using long words and well-worn phrases (copying from each other) and produce horrors of jargon. Then everyone tells you how hard it is to write, and you

lose confidence. . . . Think about the things they've written and realize that they can do no better because they don't know they're doing badly. They think they're writing English. You know it's bad because you hear the discords, not because you've parsed the sentences. That means you can hear the harmony, too, so just sit down and write. You need give no thought to the words, for the music inside will sing and it will all go down properly if you'll only *let* it and don't interfere with the flow, and if you *don't stop in the middle* and tear it up. Let the whole thing flow out and then, and *only then,* look it over and make your small improvements.

WORK HARD. But remember that the Buddhist precept "exert meticulous effort" does not mean compulsive wallowing in petty details. It means what Dickens wrote in *"David Copperfield"*—to try "with all my heart to do well . . . thorough-going, ardent, and sincere earnestness . . . never to put *one* hand to anything on which I could throw my whole self; and never to affect depreciation of my work, whatever it was."

> Writing is a matter of craft and know-how, yes, but also a matter of tenacious faith. And closely related to faith— perhaps rising from it—are all those virtues of courage, hope, steadfastness of intention, *caritas,* for the process, the journey itself.
>
> —JOANNNA HIGGINS

LANGUAGE AND STYLE:

As Fletcher Pratt said at Breadloaf Writers' Conference in 1950, there are four main technical points about writing:

"I MISS THE GOOD OLD DAYS WHEN ALL
WE HAD TO WORRY ABOUT WAS NOUNS AND VERBS."

1. Use strong words—mostly nouns and verbs—not weak.
2. When in doubt, leave it out (especially adjectives and adverbs).
3. Show, don't tell.
4. Plant it now, dig it later.

When Shakespeare wants to move you, he uses very simple words. Study Lear's recognition of Cordelia for the power of simple words. Or read the following, part of a review Isaac wrote in 1962 in *The New Leader:*

. . . [I]f the book has a flaw, it is that it continually irritates by being a shade more pretentious than it needs to be. [The author] quotes with approval Shakespeare's phrase "the multitudinous seas incarnadine" which Macbeth uses to indicate that the very ocean would not suffice to clean his bloody hand but that his hand would rather color the ocean.

The phrase quoted does indeed present the mind of the listener with the restless swell of the sea, but it is the *next* line, which he does not quote, that actually paints the colossal picture, for it goes "making the green one red." At a stroke the world is filled from horizon to horizon with blood—and it is done in the simplest Anglo-Saxon.

There is a lesson here for many liberals who (owing perhaps to boyhood traumas) can never sufficiently believe in their own education and intelligence and must constantly spread the evidence out on white paper in the form of words too long, sentences too weighted, ideas too jammed. It is for this reason, perhaps, that liberals carry less weight in the world than the worthiness of their cause deserves. It would seem at times that they speak only to each other, and listen, in rapt admiration, only to themselves. . . .

16

Style does not consist of verbiage any more than a corsage consists of ribbon. The wealth of the English language is great and a long, rare, or specialized word has its place where no other word will do. It is the essence of style, however, to know when no other word will do and not to succumb otherwise. Where the short and simple constructions make the point, they must be used—particularly if you are trying to persuade and educate others and are not merely lulling yourself to soft slumber with the lovely murmur of your own words . . .

Those who write clearly have readers; those who write obscurely have commentators.

—ALBERT CAMUS

No one can write decently who is distrustful of the reader's intelligence, or whose attitude is patronizing.

—E. B. WHITE

He who is afraid to use an "I" in his writing will never make a good writer.

—LIN YUTANG

It takes less time to learn how to write nobly than how to write lightly and straightforwardly.

—NIETZSCHE

. . . It is the business of the writer to hide the fact that writing is his business. Readers are not interested in the mechanics of authorship.

—A. A. MILNE

[From an unpublished letter by both of us to an editor] We feel that even young readers are smart enough to know who is talking without each and every speech identified as to speaker. Readers who don't understand our sentence construction or our humor are the sort of readers who won't read any book without illustrations that isn't based on a previously seen TV show or movie.

We also prefer to use "said" as often as possible instead of other words. Readers don't notice the word "said" but other words intrude upon the smooth transfer of dialogue from the page to the reader's mind.

. . . The fiction writer's most precious tool is the illusion that what he is describing actually happened. The past tense helps sweep us away in the story; the present tense subtly reminds us that it is artifice after all. . . . To describe an event in the past tense means taking a kind of responsibility for it; the I-Am-a-Camera present tense gives the unearned illusion of pure objectivity. It also obscures a highly questionable assumption: that, merely because something occurred and a reporter happened to see it, it is significant.
—BEN YAGODA

Past tense narrative is the voice we use when we want to be believed. Present tense is . . . phony, distracting, and elitist. . . . Elitist devices. . . . interfere with the storyteller's ability to communicate with the audience. . . . The storytellers who shape the conscience of the people invariably speak the language of the people. To the degree that you use elitist devices, you abdicate the storyteller's throne.
—ORSON SCOTT CARD

Details call things into being.
—S. LEONARD RUBINSTEIN

Descriptive language should be suitable to the subject of the story and sound neither forced nor out of place. The object

CULTURE POLICE

of all writing . . . is to get the reader to turn the page, and the reader will turn pages more quickly if he feels an empathy for the characters, or the situation, or the locale he is reading about.

—ROBERT L. FISH

The Two Ways of Writing Fiction

[From I. A.'s essay "The Mosaic and the Plate Glass"]

In one way you pay more attention to the language itself than to the events you are describing. You are anxious to write colorfully, to paint a picture of the setting or the background of the events. You wish to evoke a mood in the reader which will make it possible for him to feel the events taking place more intensely than would be possible through a mere recounting.

This is not an easy thing to do well. There have been very many colorful phrases which have been so frequently employed in the past by other writers to evoke whatever it is you are trying to evoke that they have been used up and wrung dry. They have lost all capacity to do their work. Sometimes even one use in the past knocks out a phrase if that one use is very famous because it occurs in *Hamlet* or in the Gettysburg Address.

The effort to be colorful and yet to avoid the cliché is difficult. Sometimes considerable polishing and repolishing is required to make things just right.

If you succeed, you have written poetically. You have written with style. Everyone admires you—at least, everyone with pretensions to literary taste.

And yet, though the phrases may be memorable, though the swing of the sentences may be grand, though the moods and emotions may be effectively evoked—the *story* may be just a little bit hard to understand.

Such writing is like a glorious mosaic built up out of pieces of colored glass. It may be a gorgeous spectacle and wonderful to look at, but if you're interested in seeing what's going on in the street, you're going to have a little trouble seeing through the mosaic.

Don't get me wrong. It is not necessarily important to understand something at once. In fact, brooding over a well-written mosaic of a story and rereading it may, little by little, illuminate you. You may find all kinds of symbolisms, all sorts of understandings on different levels. The fulfillment you will feel at achieving a deep understanding of something cannot be matched by surface "understanding."

If you have time for it.

Let's face it. We're not all people of leisure. And even if we have leisure sometimes, there are many activities competing for the time we have at some particular period, and we may not feel able to spend the time on a work of literature that requires all of our sustained attention. Yet we would like to read a story. What can we do?

There's another kind of writing, too.

In this other kind, words and phrases are chosen not for their freshness and novelty, or for their unexpected ability to evoke a mood, but simply for their ability to describe what is going on without themselves getting in the way. Everything is subordinated to clarity. It is the kind of writing in which the direct sentence is preferred to the involved subordinate clause, the familiar word to the unfamiliar word, and the short word to the long word.

This does not mean there are no involved subordinate clauses and no unfamiliar or long words. It does mean that these devices are used only when it is necessary to do so for clarity. *All things being equal,* you plump for the direct, the familiar, the short.

21

The result is that you can see what's happening with absolute clarity (if the writing is handled well enough). Ideally, you're not even aware of the writing.

Such writing might be compared to plate glass in a window. You can see exactly what's going on in the street and you're not aware of the glass. . . .

. . .[I]t took two thousand years to progress from colored glass that made marvelous mosaics to something as simple and "nothing" as clear glass without streaks, wobbles, or bubbles. Strange that something so "simple" should be so much more technically difficult to manufacture than something "artistic."

And so it is in literature, too. Because one story is written very artistically, very poetically, very stylishly, it is easy to see that it was difficult to write and required great skill in the creation. But because another story is written so simply and clearly that you're not aware of the writing, it doesn't mean that there was no trouble in the writing at all. It may well have been more difficult to insert clarity than to insert poetry. There is a great deal of art to creating something that seems artless.

I know one writer (his initials are I.A. and I'm very close to him) who's been told on numerous occasions: "I don't know that you're exactly a writer, but you're a good story-teller."

The jackasses who say this intend to be condescending, but I smile and feel complimented, for it's not easy to tell a story well. If you don't believe that, stop people at random and ask them to tell you a story. If you keep it up for an unbroken period of as little as three hours, you may never recover your sanity.

Writing in such a fashion that the writing is unnotice-able, that the events described pass directly into your brain as though you were experiencing them yourself, is a difficult and a necessary art.

Sometimes you *want* to see what's happening in the street, and even the smallest imperfection in the glass in the window will annoy you. And sometimes you *want* to read a story and be carried along with the events rapidly and smoothly without even the smallest imperfection in the writing to remind you that you are only reading and not experiencing.

Well, then, suppose we have two stories: a mosaic and a plate glass. They are not directly comparable, to be sure, but suppose that they (each in its own way) are equally good. In that case, which should one choose? If it were I making the choice, I would plump for the plate glass every time. It's what I like to write and what I like to read.

We have become a country in which millions of people are able to express themselves in only a rudimentary way, while many of those who can do better go to almost any length to avoid being generally understood.
—EDWIN NEWMAN

You know, I've read your last story, and I ought to have returned it weeks ago. It isn't right. It's almost right. It almost works. But not quite. You are too literary. You must not be literary. Suppress all the literature and it will work.
—COLETTE to GEORGES SIMENON

Rule Seventeen. Omit needless words! Omit needless words! Omit needless words!
—WILL STRUNK, quoted by E. B. WHITE

CULTIVATE A GOOD MEMORY:
JANET (at 4 A.M.): What's the matter?

ISAAC: I've been awake for a while.

JANET: But what's the . . .

ISAAC: Nothing. I've been thinking. I woke up suddenly with a gimmick for the next Black Widower's story.

JANET: Write it down!

ISAAC: I'm going back to sleep.

JANET: But you won't remember it when you wake up!

ISAAC: I will. [he does]

WRITE THINGS DOWN:

[after we both read a novel that had vivid descriptions of horrible conditions in times past.]

ISAAC: I think that if I had any place on earth and any time in history up to now, I would choose to live here and now.

JANET: The only place to live is at the edge of the future.

ISAAC: Write that down!

JANET: What did I say?

"The horror of that moment," the King went on, "I shall never, never forget!"
"You will, though," the Queen said, "if you don't make a memorandum of it."

—LEWIS CARROLL

STILL MORE ON THE WORK:

WRITERS' MAGAZINES: The magazines on writing are valuable. They give market lists every month, up-to-date information on publishers, and, best of all, they have readable articles on writing by working writers.

MECHANICAL AIDS: There are so many arguments about various mechanical aids to writing that the only solution is to

HEMINGWAY'S DOG MEETS FAULKNER'S DOG

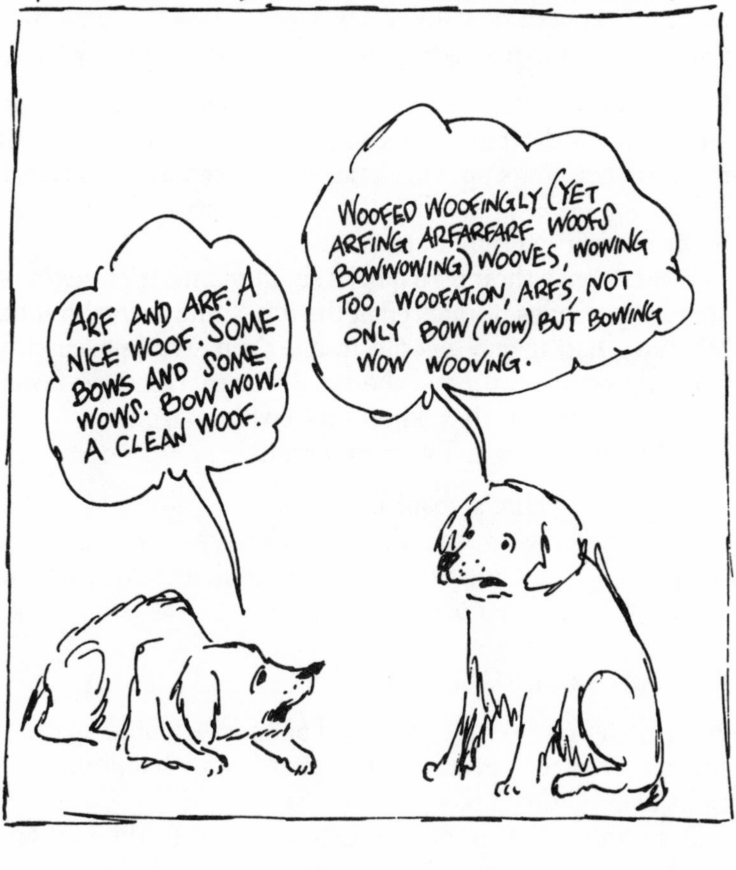

study them all, choose what seems best for you (trying it out first if possible), and then to change if it isn't.

We use both electric (not electronic) typewriters and word processors, with a nonelectric typewriter in a closet in case the power goes. Isaac writes happily with pen while on trips, exclaiming about how silent it is. Janet curses the tendonitis that reappears in her right thumb with too much handwriting.

MANUSCRIPT PAGE: Be sure to read a good technical book on writing if you don't already know how. It will teach you about margins, headings, spacing, and so on, necessary knowledge even if you never print out but send your prose on telephone wires from one computer to another.

Writers have their own quirks about manuscript pages— some want pages numbered at the top, some at the bottom. We have had to pay people to alter our word-processing software so we can have the narrower margins we favor, but we assure you that editors like wide margins.

[While watching a TV commercial]

ISAAC:	That's absurd!
JANET:	(who is reading a book) What is?
ISAAC:	It's a writer showing his manuscript—look!
JANET:	Heavens!
ISAAC:	Single-spaced!
TOGETHER:	SINGLE-SPACED!

PLOTS: All plots—which you will of course double-space— involve change, because something has to happen. Good plots also involve change *in* the protagonist.

Remember that human beings are both frightened and fascinated by change. No matter what you believe in or what you hope for, every day of existence tells you that:

REALITY=UNPREDICTABILITY=UNCERTAINTY

or to put it bluntly: REALITY=CHANGE.

If you think this is just a simple truth that everyone knows and accepts, think about the way people run away from uncertainty. Notice the rise in popularity of cults that promise certainty.

Yet people still enjoy reading about change, in the plethora of nonfiction books on the subject or in fiction that has genuine plots.

To a reader, a book is a humanly controllable way of savoring change.

When constructing plots, think of change as movement toward ultimate success (interpersonal, financial, creative) no matter how many intermediate failures stand in the way. The movement can also be toward ultimate failure, but this can be seen as success if the protagonist goes down fighting and/or learns something on the way.

In life, not just in fictional plots, we all change and we all die. Whether the change is growth, or the dying a final failure, is up to us.

3.

Coping

COPING I

You are not alone. Everyone has trouble coping. Notice that in addition to the shelves of books on the subject, coping is now a category of greeting card. This is going to be a long chapter.

One of the main things you have to cope with is that nobody understands writers. Not even other writers.

Cheer up. You are now closer in touch with the human existential problem—you are, after all, alone. BUT:

> . . . Nearly all works of creative originality are conceived in states of constructive aloneness. In fact, only the creative person who is not afraid of this constructive loneliness will have command over the productive emanations of his creative mind.
>
> —FRIEDA FROMM-REICHMAN

Coping with the life of a writer will be much easier if you take pains to read carefully and memorize our first suggestion, shortly to appear in capital letters.

The New Yorker once printed the contents of a piece of

paper found in the street where it had obviously been dropped by someone. It was a handwritten list called "Things to Do Today." Nothing had been checked off except the first item: GET STARTED.

> You live in the eternal now, a choosing one, triggering all about you into continually new patterns in this flux of choice and change. . . . Start here . . . go ahead . . . invent, experiment, take the next step . . . without dawdling or getting tied up in irrelevancies.
>
> —JOHN R. PLATT

Many writers think they can't start writing unless they have a big block of time for it. This is a mistake. *Carpe diem.*

Seize the day . . . or the minute. Your mind will pick things up quickly after an interruption of minutes or hours. If you can, set aside whole mornings (or evenings, if you're a night person) for concentrated work but develop the habit of being able to write in snatched pieces of time when you have to.

Try to have more than one writing project going. When your gorge rises at the thought of a particular project, you can turn to the other and then go back to the first refreshed.

The important thing is to get going. Pouring out the first draft as fast as possible is both exhilarating and soothing, and you feel like a functioning part of the universe.

> . . . [S]he had got her mood onto paper. . . . This is the release that all writers, even the feeblest, seek for as all men seek for love; and, having found it, they doze off happily into dreams and trouble their hearts no further.
>
> —DOROTHY L. SAYERS

THINKING is part of getting started. Learn to think creatively at odd moments, not just when you decide you have to sit down at your word processor.

Do more than one thing at a time, while thinking. Sometimes this is a little hard to do without becoming a Type A person with unpleasant physiological consequences, but it can be done.

Learn rote tasks so well that they become efficient reflexes, leaving your mind free to think. Driving a car is a perfect example of an activity that is safer and more successful after you've learned it so well you can leave it to finely tuned reflexes instead of your consciousness.

Many physical activities leave your mind free—walking is favored by many writers. Most housework, yard work, and other chores facilitate mental creativity.

Sometimes it's unnerving to have several tasks going at once—dinner cooking, the clothes washer churning, the printer printing, and you trying to balance a checkbook. If you keep an ear open for the oven timer so dinner doesn't burn, everything will be okay unless the clothes bunch to one side causing the washer to jump out of place. The printer will yell for help if it needs it. Perhaps someday washers will, too.

Spouses of writing cooks sometimes have the odd idea that said cook should use the "eyeball technique," staring at cooking food until it is done, not just barely remembering to run in from the word processor to stir something that's almost burning. Said spouses should learn to cook.

When writers seem to be doing one thing while actually writing in their heads, spouses may misinterpret facial expressions that seem to warn of medical emergencies but are only plot contortions.

We're only kidding. You don't have to agonize over

thinking. Remember that it's the one thing the human brain does best. First think of a good opening. Then think of the ending at which you'll aim. Now you've got the rudimentary structure. Relax.

Assume the plot is unfolding in your head, and listen to what your characters are saying. They know better than you do. Just write it down.

Don't be alarmed if a character seems to get out of control, whizzing off into a plot development you hadn't planned, at least consciously. This happens to the best writers and often produces great results. Shakespeare had trouble with Falstaff, who took over. Galsworthy found that Soames Forsyte developed into a hero of sorts. Doyle tried to kill off Sherlock Holmes. And Cervantes found that Sancho Panza took over both the book and the readers. Fortunately Cervantes went along with this.

> Thinking is the activity I love best, and writing to me is simply thinking through my fingers. . . . The only really human thing is the mind. I used to think about dying and worry and wish the brain could be saved, but then I put it all down on paper, every thought I've had that's worth anything, and it's there for people to read.
>
> [UNPUBLISHED LETTER: I.A.]

GET AT LEAST SOME FINANCIAL SECURITY: This should have come first in any list of advice, but it's a grim subject and we put it off.

As children of the Great Depression, we were overly impressed by the importance of having a *sure* way of making money. We both went to school seemingly forever to get careers which would guarantee a fairly steady income. This made it possible for us to write on the side and eventually full-time. And each of us started out, at age eleven, wanting only to write.

Careers that make money so you can write may also be rewarding in other ways. They certainly provide grist for the mill, especially that inestimable knowledge of being on the inside of something other people do, instead of looking at it from outside.

We admit we are biased. We stress the importance of being able to make money in some way other than writing. Then you'll never have to write what you yourself disapprove of.

And perhaps, if you're lucky, someday you'll be able to make your main living by writing.

COPING II

This part of the section on Coping is advice on improving your ability to enjoy the *job* of writing.

STAY FIT: Find and read a good book on health, nutrition, and exercise. Staying fit makes a lot of difference.

Eat right. Some people stay awake in work sessions better after a high-protein meal, since high-carbohydrate releases tryptophan to make you sleepy. Too much sugar and salt can increase salt retention, possibly raising blood pressure and bolluxing up the intracellular fluid in those brain cells you count on to do clear thinking.

Frequent small meals usually keep up energy and prevent excess weight gain. Sensible, nutritious, nonfattening meals, that is. And vitamins help many people.

We strongly disapprove of smoking. We have files of information on how it louses up thinking in addition to increasing sick time, reducing life expectancy, and preventing the Asimovs from enjoying your company.

Take mininaps when you need to. Remember that most adults don't need to sleep as much as they think they do, especially after thirty-five.

Exercise is now proven to be an antidote for fatigue and depression, particularly the kind that comes from sitting too long and fretting too much. We work out at home on an exercise machine that imitates cross-country skiing, but other writers enjoy regular visits to a gym or running in the park. Sex is also good exercise, and more fun.

As our writing friend Adam Fisher says, with exercise "the whole body feels used and the mind is in balance with the body instead of being separate."

BE ORGANIZED:This is a euphemism for being efficiently lazy, so you'll have more time to write.

Know where everything is so you won't waste time looking for something. It also helps to have one—and only one—Space For Disorganization, a shelf or drawer where things can be dumped until you have time to be neat, methodical, and are able to make decisions about where things should go. When you think you've lost something, it will probably be in the Space For Disorganization. And if you wait long enough you'll find that more of its contents can be just thrown out, and the process of doing so can serve as a Constructive Activity to Raise Self-esteem. You'll need lots of those.

Always have ample supplies of writing necessities, more than you think you'll need. Also have housekeeping and food staples so you won't have to go shopping too often for those.

Never rely on shopping as a cure for writer's block and/or depression. It's not a good escape but a trap that clutters up your life with possessions that require attention and care. Of course, some people go too far:

ISAAC: I don't need new pants. I love old things.

JANET: Please buy a new pair of pants!

ISAAC: I love you, old thing, but I hate shopping. I want to write. Here's a pair of my pants. See if you can get another like it.

JANET: But what size? It doesn't say . . .

ISAAC: I can't remember. I hope you don't have any trouble at the store, dear, while I'm finishing this scene in my novel.

[Later]

JANET: Here's your new pants. I had no trouble at the store. Just humiliation as the clerk measured your faded, ragged, baggy old pants for the size . . .

ISAAC: Thank you, dear. I see you threw the old pair in the wastebasket. Just hang them up in my closet. . . .

This brings us to a vital point: SIMPLIFY LIFE.

. . . Our life is frittered away by detail . . . simplify, simplify.
—HENRY DAVID THOREAU

. . . When one is revolving rapidly on the wheel of things there doesn't seem to be an opportunity for anything one really wants to do.
—L. M. MONTGOMERY

Focus on important things. In the nonwriting part of life there will be crises that take precedence, but in your writing life cultivate a sixth sense for what's important. For instance, if you want your children's book to be out in time for Christmas sales, get it in, even if your attempt to give birth to the Great American Novel has to be put off, or achieved in what are whimsically termed off-hours.

DON'T TRY TO BE A PERFECTIONIST. Follow Peg Bracken's rule (dimly remembered) that when you see something that should be done, do it at once. Don't plan to do it later when you think you'll be able to do it right, meaning perfectly. This goes for everything from writing a chapter to wiping off a dirty counter.

Remember that possessions do complicate living and that usually Less is More. The more complicated an apparatus is, the more trouble it is likely to be. Hand-operated can openers work when there's no electricity; surgical hemostats are simple, useful tools for many tasks; fancy food processors don't save time because you're tempted to cook complicated dishes and you have to wash the mechanism; old-fashioned file cards are often simpler and easier than doing the same thing on a computer. . . .

The measure of anyone's freedom is what he can do without.

—L. M. Montgomery

Do you want to give a lot of parties? Go to every new play and movie? Read about and make studious purchases to update equipment frequently? Redecorate the writer's manse? Answer every letter with a long one of your own? Go on a speaking tour every week? Say yes to every request for a telephone interview? Hire servants who will have to be instructed and checked on when you can do whatever it is more efficiently? Forget to pay your bills and income tax so you spend long hours catching up, sometimes in lawyers' offices?

Or do you want to write?

It's all very well to have a fascinating, full life from which you may get material for writing. But when you actually are writing, it's best to live simply and concentrate on those words coming out of your head.

In the Asimov household, there are no interesting gadgets, games, costumes, or even skeletons in our closets, only typewriters. We can't understand why most people think we are a trifle strange.

Isaac (with pained expression): Whenever I have endured or accomplished some difficult task—such as watching television, going out socially, or sleeping—I always look forward to rewarding myself with the small pleasure of getting back to my typewriter and writing something. This enables me to store up enough strength to endure the next interruption.

Notes on being a Writer

[from an unpublished I.A. letter to a young writer]
The writer has always had a social prestige ever since the early days when writing was a close-kept monopoly of the learned. The creative writer was valued when he was the only means of entertainment as he plucked his lyre and sang his lays about the tribal campfire.

Each human being with the kind of spark of intelligence that finds itself fascinated by books during childhood cannot help but find it wonderful to be a writer—if only because we imagine that the writer is constantly telling himself these wonderful stories of which [the reader] gets only a poor little dribble. Think how wonderful to be Mrs. Bland [E. Nesbit] and know so much more about the Psammead than she has a chance to tell. . . .

There are, therefore, a vast number of youngsters who aspire to write and so few really do.

The trouble is that though the rewards of writing are great if achieved, the drudgery of writing is equally great regardless of whether the rewards are achieved or not. The writer is the slave of his writing and there are people who *will not be enslaved.*

To be a writer means to write when the weather is beautiful outside; it means to write when you could be resting or talking or visiting or doing all sorts of pleasant things; it means to write not because you are happy writing so much as that you are unhappy not writing.

And most of all, to be a writer means to write whether there is any reward or not. That is why a writer finds it so difficult to overcome the feeling of annoyance at any interference with his writing whether from a friend, from an editor, or even a person whom he loves above all else.

Of course the help is meant to improve his writing, and of course it may end by improving his writing and increasing his success. In his heart, however, he doesn't want to improve or be successful; he wants to put the material that is swelling within him on paper and the process is so individual and so private that it cannot be interfered with without spoiling it somewhat. A professional writer will make alterations when demanded, but I have never known one to do so without grumbling. . . .

Write for the pleasure of writing only, and never think of whether what you write is "good" or "bad." Do you wonder whether the echo of your footsteps is good or bad, whether the blink of your eye is good or bad? Writing is a bodily function for a writer and it is what it is.

It may be wise to give up the illusion of being a famous writer, a renowned writer—but it is never an illusion to think of being just a writer. That is a matter between yourself and yourself.

ISAAC (at the top of his voice): Please don't help me! Happiness is doing it lousy yourself.

> The greatest pleasure in life is doing what people say you cannot do.
>
> —WALTER BAGEHOT

The Prolific Writer:

[an article by I. A.]

There are grave disadvantages to being a prolific writer, and if you are seriously interested in writing, it may very well be that prolificity is the last thing you want.

To be prolific means that you must be able to write quickly, facilely, and without much concern as to what improvements you might possibly introduce if you took enough time. That is precisely what you *don't* want to do if your interest is in writing well.

To write quickly and to write well are usually incompatible attributes, and if you must choose one or the other, you should choose quality over speed every time.

But suppose you do write pretty well. Isn't it possible to write quickly and easily *too*? Surely it is legitimate to dream of that. Any writer who has perspired his way through some bit of creation, who has worked his way through endless crossings-out and crumplings, and who has ended uncertainly with something whose virtues seem to dim perceptibly as he gives it a final reading must wonder what it might feel like to dash something off between yawns, so to speak, and have it read perfectly well.

Not only will a mind-wrenching job then become simple, but you will be able to turn out many more items, charge for each one, and improve your bank balance enormously.

What do you need to achieve that?

1) YOU HAVE TO LIKE TO WRITE. Without that, everything else falls to the ground, and you will have to seek other daydreams. Prolificity isn't for you.

Mind you, I don't say you must have the urge to write or the deep ambition to write. That is not enough. Everyone who tries to write must obviously have the urge and the ambition to do so, and everyone would just love to have a finished manuscript on the desk.

What about the in-between, though? What about the actual mechanical process of scribbling on paper, or beating on typewriter keys, or speaking into a mouthpiece? If that is just an agonizing intermediate step between the original urge and the final ecstasy, then you may be a good writer, you may even be a writer of genius—but you will never be a prolific writer. No one could stand that much agony.

No, the very act of turning it out must be actively pleasurable.

2) YOU MUST NOT LIKE MUCH OF ANYTHING ELSE *BUT* WRITING.

After all, most of us are constantly torn between desires, but for the writer who wants to be prolific, there should be no room for doubt. It's writing you must want to be doing, not anything else.

If you look out at one of those perfect days, when all nature is smiling and calling to you to get out there and enjoy life, and you say, "Oh hell, I'll write tomorrow," then abandon all dreams of prolificity.

If you can look out at such a day and feel a sudden pang of apprehension that some loved one is going to come over and say, "What a perfect time for a pleasant walk" or "What a perfect time to go out and do thus-and-so!" then there's hope for you. (Frankly, what I do is keep the shades down at all times and pretend there's a blizzard outside.)

3) YOU HAVE TO HAVE SELF-ASSURANCE. If your sentences never seem perfect to you and if you are never happy unless you have revised and revised and revised until the sentence disappears altogether under the weight of erasures and interlineations, or until you have restored it full-circle to what it was originally, then how can you hope to be prolific?

You may ask, "But what if the sentence isn't good? I just can't leave it, can I?"

Of course not, but the assumption here is that you're a

41

reasonably good writer to begin with and that it's your dream to be prolific also. As a reasonably good writer, you have undoubtedly written a reasonably good sentence, so let it go. Once you are finished with the piece, you can go over it and change anything that really *needs* changing, and then type the whole thing over to get clean copy. But then, that's it.

Remember, change only what *needs* changing. You must cultivate an active dislike for changing and never do it without a sigh of regret.

Undoubtedly, you have read over and over again that there is no such thing as writing, only rewriting; that it's the polish that does it. Sure, but that's if you want to be a *great* writer. We're talking prolific here.

4) NEVER LOSE TIME. You can replace money if you lose a wallet. You can buy a new typewriter if your apartment is ransacked. You can marry again if a divorce overtakes you. But that minute that has vanished unnecessarily will never come back, and what's more, it was the best minute you will ever have, for all future minutes will come when you are older and more nearly worn out.

There are a variety of ways of saving time, and every prolific writer chooses his own. Some become completely asocial, tearing the phone out of the wall and never answering mail. Some establish a family member as dragon to stand between themselves and the world. Some turn off their senses and learn to write while activity swirls all about them.

My own system is to do everything myself. I have no assistants, no secretaries, no typists, no researchers, no agents, no business managers. My theory is that all such people waste your time. In the time it takes to explain what you want, to check what they do, to point out where they did it wrong—you can do at least three times as much by yourself.

So there you are. If you want to be a prolific writer, you have to be a single-minded, driven, nonstop person. Sounds horrible, doesn't it?

Well, then, concentrate on being a *good* writer, and leave prolific for those poor souls who can't help it.

The responsibility of the writer is to observe, listen, and record. Then he tells a story, adding imagination to experience, and it bares the scars of his soul.
—JOHN LE CARRE

An epitome of my life: my first book ends (designedly) with the word "explained"—my last with the word "unknown."
—OLIVER WENDELL HOLMES

. . . who also said:

Realize life as an end in itself. . . . I wonder if cosmically an idea is any more important than the bowels.

If you would only recognize that life is hard, things would be so much easier for you.
—LOUIS D. BRANDEIS

MEDICAL ADVICE
[JANET]

Don't worry.
So it starts that way—a rumble inside,
A feeling of faintness and doom.
Don't take a cathartic,
Or sedative, tranquilizer, umbrage.
Let it come, yelling at light of day.
Don't blame the cerebral cortex.
Words sneakily slink along synapses
Laced into primitive pathways,
Churning up hypothalamic cells, gathering strength
    and purpose,
Pushing in rhythms reticular,
Producing feedback, tension,
Half-formed thoughts that reek of dire import.
Form them, damn you!
Let your snobbish cortex tremble, thinking itself
    above all that.
Even precise Popean couplets
Probably started lower down.
Don't call it a sickness.
Remember the chants in the smoky cave,
The firelight changing the painted mammoth
To a monster breathing, living in the song,
The symbol,
The word.

COPING III

The best advice on writing is: FINISH WHAT YOU WRITE. SEND IT TO EDITORS (Never to other writers).

But suppose you are too upset or depressed to finish?

Suppose you are too upset or depressed to start again once something has been rejected—or even when it's gone off to an editor at last?

How do you cope?

There are books and books on self-help, and there are many helpers, some highly trained and some not, out there in the real world. Use them if necessary.

In the meantime, remember that:

SIN IS TO HAVE LIVED WITHOUT RELATING ONESELF TO THE WORLD BY MEANS OF ONE'S HUMAN POWERS.
—ERICH FROMM

By now you've either gone to your typewriter or you feel horribly guilty. It's difficult to be creative in spite of the general cussedness of life, but it gets easier once you realize that creativity is a marvelous way to transcend life's little problems—like threats of war and terrorism, economic chaos, intimations of mortality, and the sneaking feeling that you have accomplished absolutely nothing all week.

Don't catastrophize. It will increase your problems. Ask any writer, who's generally good at it.

As Charles Schulz had Charlie Brown say, it's better if you "try to dread only one day at a time."

Just live one day at a time. However unhappy you are you can still act your part for one more day. And as for trust, well, that's what wins it. People like to know that whatever happens they can rely on you to play your part.

—ELIZABETH GOUDGE

It really pays to try to be as civilized, self-aware, and mature as you can possibly manage. Contrary to popular opinion, creativity does not spring from angry, bleeding egos steeped in permanent misery. Maturity, self-awareness, and peace of mind free you to be creative.

Instead of self-pity, try compassion. Self-pity alienates you from the human race. You feel superior in the uniqueness of suffering, which "they" are supposed to notice and do something about. But compassion makes you feel connected to others and lets you forgive, laugh at, and help yourself.

Being productively creative is a sure way of getting happy, but remember being happy improves creativity, which is stifled when you drown yourself in the negative aspects of life. Research has shown that deliberately thinking of pleasant things and altering your facial musculature to a smile does change the way your brain works. Endorphins increase, your thinking clears, and hope rises.

The bigger one thing is, the smaller it makes another thing. The more you pile on the happiness heap, the smaller the unhappiness heap looks in comparison.

—ELIZABETH GOUDGE

Not everyone agrees:

Although an extreme case is to be avoided, a little melancholy goes a long way toward thinking intelligently about life and literature. The well-tempered melancholic knows better, for example, than to be taken in by absolute answers or elaborately rigged philosophical systems. His self-absorption insulates him from political and cultural demagoguery. Not for him the cultivation of a public *tristesse* merely to appear interesting. No, the melancholic's pessimism is private and impartial, embracing the fate of snails and nations. And unlike those who place hope in God or man, he is never disappointed.

—ARTHUR KRYSTAL

And after that, we need Sean O'Casey:

Our world has beauty and our life has hope. In spite of the despair of the beats and wailers, the harp in the air still sings the melody of hope.

And William James:

Be not afraid of life—believe that life is worth living and your belief will help create the fact.

[JANET] Attitude is all. Years ago when I worked in a plastic surgery clinic as a psychiatrist, I interviewed a middle-aged housewife due for a rhinoplasty. At the six-month follow-up session, she reported that since her nose job she'd tried all sorts of new things and found life much more enjoyable. Then she burst into tears and said, "but I could have done them with my old nose instead of waiting all these years!"

You don't want to go on unless you are assured of success? Of having every review favorable, every sale leading to a bestseller? You decide not to be happy because the readers (or teachers or critics or editors or relatives) don't love you enough? As the psychoanalyst and writer Clara Thompson said, "If you want unconditional enthusiasm and love, get a dog."

People can write under appalling circumstances. Remember Mrs. Trollope, Anthony's mother. He said:

47

Her power of dividing herself into two parts, and keeping her intellect by itself clear from the troubles of the world, and fit for the duty it had to do, I never saw equalled. I do not think that the writing of a novel is the most difficult task which a man may be called upon to do; but it is a task that may be supposed to demand a spirit fairly at ease. The work of doing it with a troubled spirit killed Sir Walter Scott. My mother went through it unscathed in strength, though she performed all the work of day-nurse and night-nurse to a sick household . . . for there were soon three of them dying.

. . . [T]hough personal suffering can seem to a man an entirely lonely and isolating thing, a prison within a prison, it is in actual fact the exact opposite. Through it he reaches the only real unity, oneness with the whole of suffering creation.

—Elizabeth Goudge

Each individual life alters the nature of human nature. The extraordinary thing that experience brings is that in adjusting one's hopes and wishes to bitter reality they often take on a better strength than one could have hoped to expect. Often many of the worst things that happen to a person become the means to a discovery of which one would otherwise be quite blind.

—Jeffrey Smith

Isaac (on the train): To avoid thinking bad thoughts on trips I can always amuse myself by planning what I'm going to write when I get back to my typewriter. Shall I continue writing my history of the world where Columbus just

"OH, HOW I HATE THE RE-WRITING!"

	discovered America on page 750 or shall I work some more on my Bible book where Noah's ark is floating on the flood? Or shall I put the most recent Black Widowers into final copy . . .
JANET:	But your novel . . .
ISAAC:	. . . or should I write my next *F&SF* article or my next editorial for *Asimov's* or should I do the intelligent thing and write my energy piece at a buck a word with only two weeks to deadline?
JANET:	Isaac, we're on a trip. Life is a journey, you know.
ISAAC:	Life is a journey, but don't worry, you'll find a parking place at the end.

[From an unpublished I.A. letter]: We all have our illusions . . . thrice happy he who can abandon them cheerfully in time to exploit the actual with efficiency. But if that is not possible, then it is still something to be able to abandon them under any circumstances. . . .

Burns laments that the mouse whose nest he turned up with his plow is concerned only with present sorrow while he himself can look back with grief and forward with dread.

Homo sapiens alone of all the known objects in the universe can look forward to an inevitable death; he alone can look back with regret; he alone can sigh for the might-have-beens. It is the penalty of being human. Shall we accept the gifts of being human—the consciousness of beauty, the exaltation of abstractions, the knowledge that makes gods of us—and not accept the penalty too?

[ISAAC] If my doctor told me I had only six months to live, I wouldn't brood. I'd type a little faster.

WRITER'S BLOCK

We gave up on including a large section on the etiology, diagnosis, and treatment of WRITER'S BLOCK. Everyone knows that at least one of us doesn't get writer's block.

Each person's block is highly individual, so you'll have to track down the causes of your own and experiment to see what helps get you out of it.

Everyone seems to have a different method, and we've already stated ours—work on more than one thing at a time.

Some of the writers we interviewed said writer's block doesn't exist, that the term covers up procrastination, self-indulgence, attention-getting, and "trying to mystify the business." Others said that if you've once learned to write on deadline you don't have time for writer's block (although some still get it when the deadline is their own, not that of a job imposed by someone else).

According to Hemingway and other writers, block can be prevented by quitting for the day when on the rise—in the middle, not at the end of a scene when you'd have to start cold the next day.

Creative flow is induced in many writers by the act of turning on the computer, and when the flow stops temporarily it can be restarted after a break to listen to music, watch baseball on TV, read (or watch) comfortingly familiar stories. Reading mysteries seems to be a favorite break (unless you write them)—"if the stories are focused, clear, and logical, to help me refocus on what I'm doing."

Good "battery chargers" can be solitary meditation, or talking to friends (but not about writing).

Writers usually say that when you feel as if you can't write what you want the way you want, it's best to "write it all out even if you think it's garbage. Then put it away, do something else, and go back to sort it out."

Did you ever have writer's block? It

If you are in difficulties with a book, try the element of surprise; attack it at an hour when it isn't expecting it.

—H. G. WELLS

To write that essential book, the only true book, a great writer does not need to invent it . . . since it already exists in each of us, but merely to translate it. The duty and task of a writer are those of a translator.

—MARCEL PROUST

What one has learned must be passed on or life is nothing. At least one must try to pass it on.

—ANON.

We do not discover a life that is already laid out for us. We cut our own path. We create our own selves. . . . We can discover the meanings of life by finding the tasks which are uniquely our own.

—SHELDON ACKLEY

Mankind is a part of nature beginning to understand itself . . . with an inalienable prerogative of responsibility which we cannot devolve . . . even upon the stars. We can share it only with each other.

—SIR CHARLES SHERRINGTON

Live now; accept yourself as you are now. There is no one to be always blamed, no one to be always praised.

—STEWART W. HOLMES

Accept the fact that writers do sometimes surpass themselves, and that the most unlikely might bring off a masterpiece one day, as it were, by accident.

—A. A. MILNE

Creativity, like love, should be diagnosed retrospectively.

—JOHN L. SCHIMEL

"I'VE GOTTEN QUITE A BIT OUT OF THAT CREATIVE WRITING CLASS. I THINK I'LL BECOME A LITERARY AGENT."

OH, WELL

Still discouraged?

Do you feel that your writer's block is hopeless?

Worse, do you feel more than uncertain about the desirability of coping with the writer's life—that is, with life as a person who writes?

Maybe writing isn't your form of creativity.

That's all right. There are many kinds of creativity to be enjoyed:

Her creativeness found its joy in the shaping of everyday life to a form of comeliness, so that it became not just something that one put up with but something that was enjoyable and lovely in itself.

ELIZABETH GOUDGE

4

Editing and Reacting to Editors

No passion on earth, neither love nor hate, is equal to the passion to alter someone else's draft.

—H. G. WELLS

Wells was right, and because he was, we urge all writers to try editing someone else's work now and then. You may find yourself behaving just like the editors you have always condemned. You'll also learn about writing and have more sympathy for those editors who tackle your own stuff often with such astonishing reasonableness.

But don't expect yourself—or any writer—to be astonishingly reasonable when you get back your manuscript full of corrections, comments, and queries.

JANET: I don't understand the editor's comment here.

ISAAC: Don't complain. That's a polite comment. A mere query, not even rude. Once I wrote under a copy editor's query, "Your job is to be erudite, not sarcastic." The editor actually apologized!

JANET: But I don't think I can answer this . . .

ISAAC: And then there was the time that an editor wrote in the margin "I don't understand this" and I wrote "I do."

JANET: And here they've criticized my grammar. I suppose they're right—are they?

ISAAC: Yes. Editors usually are, unless you're *trying* to write bad grammar and they compulsively correct it. But when they're right I usually write

> "thank you," and I let it pass when they valiantly try to rearrange my frequently Germanic word order into English.

JANET: That's nice, dear, but here my interesting word has been replaced by a dull one . . .

ISAAC: Don't let editors edit the life out of your sentences!

JANET: It's amazing that editors all seem to love you.

ISAAC: I like them. I'm funny that way.

But sometimes the editor-writer relationship goes awry, as shown in the following I.A. letter written many years ago:

[The book manuscript] came back completely rewritten and retyped, the work taking him exactly eighty-two hours, as [the editor] carefully explains. His memo is very flattering to me and comments on my "original and brilliant" idea and says "we have never before published a [that series book] which contained so sophisticated and complex a structure." . . . He also points out that he has edited many famous writers.

The only difficulty is that he has simply crossed out my style and substituted his own. My style is as spare and informal as it is possible for a style to be. It is almost conversational. His is much more formal.

For instance (and I swear I picked this out at random), I write, concerning Benjamin Franklin's effect on the French aristocrats: "He charmed them all, and all they wanted to do was to help the old man and his country." He changes it to "He charmed them; and presto, they wanted to do anything they could to help the old man and his young country."

Now in my sentence, the beginning, "He charmed them all, and all . . . " is a useful repetition. It lends a lulling quality which somehow gives the feeling of the almost hypnotic effect Franklin had upon the French. (No, I didn't do it purposely; but my intuition did.) [The editor] breaks it up with two full stops: "He charmed them/and presto/" and the two breaks are choppy and unhypnotic. Besides, I never use the word "presto" and it offends my ears when it presumes to represent my writing.

Again he changed "the old man and his country" to "the old man and his young country." You may think this is an insignificant change but it isn't. In the phrase, "the old man and his country" there is only one accent mark and it is on man. It reads "the old MAN and his country." That is how it should be. The aristocrats were in love with the MAN and his country was loved only for the connection with the man.

In [the editor's] phrase there are two accents and they are on the adjectives—"the OLD man and his YOUNG country"—and there is no sense in contrasting the ages. It has no significance in this context.

All through [the editor] supplies more precise, more formal phraseology, but he has no ear and damn it, I have.

. . . My problem is how do I tell the editor that he ought not to have rewritten my book. After all, he meant well and worked hard and spent eighty-two hours at it.

Here's another place (random, I swear). I wrote "They called themselves the 'Green Mountain boys' and they were after Fort Ticonderoga . . . " He changed it to "They called themselves the 'Green Mountain boys' and their hope was to conquer Fort Ticonderoga."

There's no question that "they were after" is colloquial and "their hope was to conquer" is the proper accurate way of phrasing it, but Ethan Allen's boys *were* colloquial. They were wild farmboys without discipline or organization who would never have said that they were "hoping to conquer." They would have said they "were after" it and added a few salty curse words, too.

The sound is as important as the words, and it is wrong to try to describe an informal situation with formal sounds. The reader will never believe your words when they are contradicted by the sounds.

[In the next letter] He badgered and badgered me about accepting his version and I remained adamant. I explained that I wanted MY book and not HIS book and that the question as to which version was better written was irrelevant. So the book will be published by [the publishing house] independently and not as part of the [editor's] series.

I feel rather bad about sticking to my guns because it makes me sound like a damned temperamental writer and I'm pretty temperamental about sounding untemperamental. I've thrown many a fit at any editorial suggestion that I'm the kind of writer who throws fits.

But really, I don't think I'm the best writer in the world, and I'm ready to accept changes. I went through the manuscript and adopted at least one hundred of the ten thousand changes he put in, where the changes actually corrected me in matters of fact, or where he really did catch me in what I like to call an "infelicity of phrasing." However, my general writing style must be inviolate, not because it is perfect but because it is the only style to which I want my name attached.

[Isaac wrote about an editor in his essay "The Campbell Touch"]: To help as John Campbell helped [young writers] takes more than a decision to do so. It takes genius to know *how,* and a sense of dedication to the task, and a glowing happiness at feeling yourself mold a fresh young talent. You have to want to fiddle with the works of new writers more than with your own. You have to joy and glory in the progress of new writers so intensely that that progress is its own reward even if the writer (all too often, but never in my case) forgets how much the help meant.

He was a genius.

I asked him once, not too long before his death, what his secret was. He said, "I have a talent that can't be taught."

"What is that?" I asked.

He said, "An eighteen-year-old named Isaac Asimov came to my office once with a story. I talked to him and read his story and found it to be impossible. From that impossible story, though, I could tell that if he were willing to work at it, he would become a good writer."

And that's what takes genius—because I certainly didn't know that about myself at the time.

All I knew was that I wanted to write. *He* knew, and on the slenderest evidence, that I *could* write.

How to React When Rejected by an Editor

First remember George Scither's rule: "We don't reject writers; we reject pieces of paper with typing on them."

Then scream a little.

[From I.A.'s essay "Rejection Slips"] Most writers kick and scream and there isn't any reason why you shouldn't, either, if it makes you feel better. However, once you are quite done with the kicking and screaming, sit down and reread the story in the light of anything [the editor] may have told you and see if you can find out what's wrong, how to correct that wrong, and how to avoid that wrong in the future. If the rejection teaches you something, you may in the long run have gained more from it than from a too-easy acceptance of a flawed story.

Don't stay mad and decide you are the victim of incompetence and stupidity. If you do, you'll learn nothing and you'll never become a writer. . . .

Don't get huffy because you have already made sales and therefore feel that no editor dare reject you. That's just not so. He *can* reject you and he need not even offer any reason. I've made nearly two thousand sales of all kinds, and I still get rejections now and then, and some pretty off-handed ones at times, too. . . .

Don't make the opposite mistake and decide the story is worthless. Editors differ and so do tastes and so do magazines' needs. Try the story somewhere else. . . . What doesn't fit one magazine might easily fit another.

5

What Writers Go Through

[from I.A.'s essay of the same title] . . . First, let me make it clear what I mean by "writers." I don't want to confine the word only to those who are successful, who have published best-selling books, or who crank out reams of published material every year (if not every day), or who make a lavish living out of their pens, typewriter, or word processors, or who have gained fame and adulation.

I also mean those writers who just sell an occasional item, who make only a bit of pin money to eke out incomes earned mainly in other fashions, whose names are not household words, and who are not recognized in the street.

In fact, let me go further and say I even mean those writers who never sell anything, who are writers only in the sense that they work doggedly at it, sending out story after story, and living in a hope that is not yet fulfilled.

We can't dismiss this last classification as "failures" and not "real" writers. For one thing, they are not necessarily failures forever. Almost every writer, before he becomes a success, even a runaway supernova success, goes through an apprentice period when he's a "failure."

Secondly, even if a writer is destined always to be a

failure, and even if he is never going to sell, he remains a human being for whom all the difficulties and frustrations of a writer's life exist and, in fact, exist without the palliative of even an occasional and minor triumph.

If we go to the other extreme and consider the writer whose every product is an apparently sure sale, we find that the difficulties and frustrations have not disappeared. For one thing, no number of triumphs, no amount of approval, seems to have any carrying power at the crucial moment.

When even the most successful writer sits down before a blank piece of paper, he is bound to feel that he is starting from scratch and, indeed, that the Damoclean sword of rejection hangs over him. (By the way, when I say "he" and "him" I mean to add "she" and "her" every time.)

If I may use myself as an example, I always wince a little when anyone, however sincerely and honestly, assumes that I am never rejected. I admit that I am rarely rejected, but between "rarely" and "never" there is a vast gulf. Even though I no longer work on spec and write only when a particular item is requested, I *still* run the risk. The year doesn't pass without at least one failure. It was only a couple of months ago that [a magazine] ordered a specific article from me. I duly delivered it; and they just as duly handed it back.

That is the possibility all of us live with. We sit here alone, pounding out the words, with our heart pounding in time. Each sentence brings with it a sickening sensation of not being right. Each page keeps us wondering if we are moving in the wrong direction.

Even if, for some reason, we feel we *are* getting it right

and that the whole thing is singing with operatic clarity, we are going to come back to it the next day and reread it and hear only a duck's quacking.

It's torture for every one of us.

Then comes the matter of rewriting and polishing; of removing obvious flaws (at least, they seem obvious, but are they really?) and replacing them with improvements (or are we just making things worse?). There's simply no way of telling if the story is being made better or is just being pushed deeper into the muck until the time finally comes when we either tear it up as hopeless or risk the humiliation of rejection by sending it off to an editor.

Once the story is sent off, no amount of steeling oneself, no amount of telling oneself over and over that it is sure to be rejected, can prevent one from harboring that one wan little spark of hope. Maybe—Maybe—

The period of waiting is refined torture in itself. Is the editor simply not getting round to it, or has he read it and is he suspended in uncertainty? Is he going to read it again and *maybe* decide to use it—or has it been lost, or has it been tossed aside to be mailed back at some convenient time and been forgotten?

How long do you wait before you write a query letter? And if you do write a letter, is it subservient enough? Sycophantic enough? Grovelling enough? After all, you don't want to offend him. He might be just on the point of accepting; and if an offensive letter from you comes along, he may snarl and rip your manuscript in two, sending you the halves.

And when the day comes that the manila envelope appears in the mail, all your mumbling that it is sure to come will not avail you. The sun will go into eclipse.

65

It's been over forty years since I've gone through all this in its full hellishness, but I remember it with undiminished clarity.

And then even if an editor's interest is aroused, you have to withstand the editor's suggestions which, at the very least, mean you have to turn back to the manuscript, work again, add or change or subtract material, and perhaps produce a finished product that will be so much worse than what had gone before that you lose the sale you thought you had made. At the worst, the changes requested are so misbegotten from your standpoint that they ruin the whole story in your eyes; and yet you may be in a position where you dare not refuse, so that you must maim your brainchild rather than see it die. (Or ought you to take back the story haughtily and try another editor? And will the first editor then blacklist you?)

Even after the item is sold and paid for and published, the triumph is rarely unalloyed. The number of miseries that might still take place are countless. A book can be produced in a slipshod manner or it can have a repulsive book jacket, or blurbs that give away the plot or clearly indicate that the blurb writer didn't follow the plot.

A book can be nonpromoted, treated with indifference by the publisher and therefore found in no bookstores, and sell no more than a few hundred copies. Even if it begins to sell well, that can be aborted when it is reviewed unsympathetically or even viciously by someone with no particular talent or qualifications in criticism.

If you sell a story to a magazine you may feel it is incompetently illustrated, or dislike the blurb, or worry about misprints. You are even liable to face the unsympathetic comments of individual readers who will wax merry,

"LOOK AT THE BRIGHT SIDE. IF YOUR BOOK WAS A BEST SELLER, ALL THESE TREES WOULD HAVE BEEN CUT DOWN FOR PAPER."

sardonic, or contemptuous at your expense—and what are *their* qualifications for doing so?

You will bleed as a result. I never met a writer who didn't bleed at the slightest unfavorable comment, and no number of favorable or even ecstatic remarks will serve as a styptic pencil.

In fact, even total success has its discomforts and inconveniences. There are, for instance:

People who send you books to autograph and return, but don't bother sending postage or return envelopes, reducing you to impounding their books or (if you can't bring yourself to do that) getting envelopes, making the package, expending stamps, and possibly even going to the post office.

People who send you manuscripts to read and criticize (nothing much, just a page-by-page analysis, and if you think it's all right, would you get it published with a generous advance, please? Thank you.).

People who dash off two dozen questions, starting with a simple one like: What in your opinion is the function of science fiction and in what ways does it contribute to the welfare of the world, illustrating your thesis with citations from the classic works of various authors. (Please use additional pages, if necessary.)

People who send you a form letter, with your name filled in (misspelled), asking for an autographed photograph, and with no envelope or postage supplied.

Teachers who flog a class of thirty into each sending you a letter telling you how they liked a story of yours, and sending you a sweet letter of her own asking you to send a nice answer to each one of the little dears.

And so on . . .

Well, then, why write?

A seventeenth-century German chemist, Johann Joachim Becher, once wrote: "The chemists are a strange class of mortals, impelled by an almost insane impulse to seek their pleasure among smoke and vapor, soot and flame, poisons and poverty; yet among all these evils I seem to live so sweetly, that may I die if I would change places with the Persian King."

Well, what goes for chemistry, goes for writing. I know all the miseries, but somewhere among them is happiness. I can't easily explain where it is or what it consists of, but it is there. I know the happiness and I experience it, and I will not stop writing while I live—and may I die if I would change places with the President of the United States.

6

Promotion

The Asimov theory of self-promotion is simple: Promotion is like pollination. It's supposed to increase the fertility of sales. Perhaps some of it does.

Wind pollination (i.e. casting the pollen outward blindly in the hope that it will occasionally land where it should): When on a TV or radio talk show, count yourself lucky if your name is pronounced properly and the host doesn't try to make a fool of you. If the host is a celebrity, don't expect your book to have been read, and be grateful if the host seems even half as interested in you as in himself or herself. You will be seen or heard by many people, but most of them don't care about you and don't read anyway.

Insect pollination (i.e. placing each bit of pollen on a useful spot): You sign books in bookstores, or after lectures, (especially to undergraduate audiences, a speaker's delight). Not as many people will see you as on TV, but those who ask you to sign books are interested in you. Best of all, they will probably read your books and tell their friends.

There's a corollary to the Asimov theory. All self-promotion is more effective if you practice the art of cheerful self-appreciation, as perfected by I.A.:

[in the supermarket checkout line]

TOTAL STRANGER: I didn't know geniuses ate.

ISAAC: This is for my wife. I don't eat.

INTERVIEWER: Are you recognized on the street?

ISAAC: Yesterday I was recognized by five people and one took a photograph. Today I was recognized by only two and I felt anonymous.

FAN: Unlike Von Daniken, your books are intellectually solvent.

ISAAC: Oh, I like that phrase.

FAN: That's a tactful way of putting it.

FAN: Your books made college so much easier for me!

ISAAC: I feel deprived. I had to do all my college work myself without my books to help me!

JANET: I absolutely adore you.

ISAAC: As well you should.

JANET: Narcissist!

ISAAC: In my case I don't consider narcissism a disease but an expression of good taste.

[At the Explorers' Club]

MEMBER: I heard you were a genius.

ISAAC: I still am.

[During lifeboat drill on a cruise ship]

OFFICER: Remember that it's women and children first.

ISAAC: And geniuses.

YOUTH: *Young* geniuses.

JANET: Do you mind that I keep saying you're cute?
ISAAC: I don't mind. What's true is true.

[The Department of Cheerful Self-appreciation's Poetry Division]
Our Isaac's a speaker of fame
With letters right after his name—
   He's the best you will see,
   Ask him, her, or *me*—
You'll find that I'll tell you the same.

JANET: That's a remarkably egotistical . . .
ISAAC: The title of the limerick is "No False Modesty."
JANET: Oh, well. What's true is true.

7

Critics

Professional literary criticism is performed by human beings. They have individual knowledge and tastes in literature, in addition to personal motivations and prejudices, philosophies, loves, and hates. They are not infallible. Nothing, not even the most apparently objective science, can be totally separated from the human being who's doing it.

That's why we think writers should not review books that directly compete with their own. Unfortunately editors of review journals and newspapers think otherwise.

If you have to be a critic, try to be as helpful as possible to the potential reader and to the author whose life is quivering in your hands. Remember what Lord Chesterfield said:

> Wrongs are often forgiven, but contempt never is. Our pride remembers it forever.

Laugh and go on writing if you are on the receiving end of a scathing review, even one written by someone you suspect of conducting a personal vendetta against you. The reviewer may only be stupid, or self-serving, or have been instructed by an editor to make all reviews scathing. Or perhaps the review is justified and you'll learn something. Perhaps.

While most writers think of critics as people who sit at the rim of creativity and throw the venom of their envy at the creators, try to be charitable toward all critics, if only to keep your blood pressure down. Notice that a favorable review is not only soothing to your physiology but impresses you with the intelligence and integrity of the reviewer.

Criticism of your work is much the same as criticism of yourself, you know, your work being an extension of yourself, and there's nothing like good slashing personal criticism for begetting humility. A conceited man never yet made a good artist. How could he? Satisfied, you stick where you are.

—ELIZABETH GOUDGE

I am afraid humility to genius is as an extinguisher to a candle.

—WILLIAM SHENSTONE

ISAAC (crying after reading Robert Burns): His poetry always makes me cry. That's my definition of art. If it makes you cry, it must be what the critics say is bad. If it makes you throw up, the critics say it's good.

And then there's I.A. as critic (in a 1963 letter to the author of an academic paper):
Thank you for sending me a reprint of your article . . . the reading of which recalled to my mind a story about St. Augustine. He was asked, "What was God doing in the days before he created heaven and earth?"
To which St. Augustine thundered the answer, "Creating hell, for such as ask questions like that."
The question to St. Augustine's mind betokened a skeptical nature, since to the truly faithful such a question would not occur. And for skeptics there was, to St. Augustine, but one end.

Your paper is an answer to the question, "How may a portion of mankind hope to profit by deliberately bringing about the destruction of most or all of the rest of mankind?"

I'm sorry, but I find this to be an inadmissible question. Regardless of your mathematics, the only answer possible is that there can be no profit, and I'm sorry you had to ask the question at all.

Since I am not St. Augustine, I will not threaten you with hellfire.

VERY TRULY YOURS. . .

This letter turned out to be false criticism, the result of misreading—the kind that authors assume critical critics always do. In this case, the author of the academic paper received a resounding apology.

Wouldn't it be wonderful if critics always apologized when they were wrong?

And finally, there's the Asimov method of reacting to adverse criticism, whether from professional critics or from readers in so-called fan mail and letters-to-the-editor columns:

Never vent your spleen in phone calls. It's hard to take back words that have been uttered.

Don't read more than the first paragraph of something unfavorable. Discard entire thing.

Or (if you did read it) follow the exact sequence of actions below:

1. Groan and scream. Read it to adoring spouse. Let adoring spouse groan and scream and mutter threats.
2. Write exceedingly vitriolic letter calculated to send unpleasant critic into emotional and intellectual shock from which there is, hopefully, no recovery.

"NOT BAD, FOR A FIRST NOVEL."

3. Read vitriolic letter to adoring spouse. Chuckle. Listen to adoring spouse laugh fiendishly.
4. Put vitriolic letter into envelope, address it, and put a STAMP on it.
5. Then tear up entire envelope several times and throw into wastebasket.

Be sure to follow this sequence precisely, and never leave out number 5.

In a 1980 reply to a fan, I. A. wrote what may be the only way to end this book's chapter on criticism:

. . .[E]very author should be judged by his readers, and I am proud of mine.

8

Words vs. Pictures

You can make a great deal of money writing for movies and television, or having your fiction bought by the same. It's no wonder that most young writers try to write screenplays, or that most novelists dicker for publishing contracts that include sales to movies and television.

If one of your stories is made into a movie and it makes your name more famous, the rest of your printed work may sell much better. Unfortunately, the credits may have in very small print "From a story by . . . " and if the ads don't mention you and the reviews don't notice the original author, you will remain unknown. If the reviews are terrible, you may be glad.

The authors of this book have practically no experience with the problem of breaking into the "visual media," and we wish the best of luck to all of you who are trying it. We also hope you won't be disappointed by your dealings with Hollywood et al., or by what happens to your words when translated into visual imagery by someone else.

Having no experience doesn't mean we don't think about it:

Book Into Movie
[From an I.A. introduction]

When a story, with its plot and its characters, appears in more than one form, you tend to be imprinted by the first form in which you experience it.

Thus I read Hugh Lofting's *Dr. Dolittle* novels beginning at the age of 10, and I read them over and over. When the movie *Dr. Dolittle* was made I absolutely and resolutely refused to see it. Why? Because Dr. Dolittle in the book, according to description and illustration, was a short and pudgy fellow of lower-class appearance. And who played him in the movies? Rex Harrison, the well-known tall, thin aristocrat. I refused to pay money for such a travesty.

On the other hand, I encountered Mary Poppins first in the movies and fell in love with Julie Andrews, Dick van Dyke, and all the rest. When my dear wife, Janet, tried to get me to read the Mary Poppins *books,* of which she had every well-thumbed title, I drew back in horror. The Mary Poppins illustrated didn't look at all like Julie Andrews. Janet, however, is very forceful and though I reared, bucked, and kicked, I finally read the books and fell in love with them, too. But I insist that there are two stories; Mary Poppins/movie and Mary Poppins/book; and that they have remarkably little to do with each other.

And that is, in my opinion, a key point to remember. Books and movies are two different art forms. The stage is a third. And even upon the stage the same play, presented as a musical comedy and as a nonmusical comedy, is an example of two different art forms.

Pygmalion, as Shaw wrote it and as Lerner and Loewe rewrote it, is in some ways the same play. The musical retains all of the plot and much of the dialogue that Shaw originally wrote and is a faithful adaptation indeed. And yet . . . when we watch the musical we must be prepared for, and forgive, the artificiality of having the characters break into song on the slightest pretext, with a complete orchestra appearing from nowhere. Shaw didn't have to struggle with *that*.

And we accept the musical convention. In fact, whenever I see the original play and hear Eliza say "Ow-w-w" and Higgins respond with "Heavens, what a noise!" and then *go on*, I always have the feeling of stepping off a curb I didn't know was there. What I expect at that moment is to have the orchestra strike up while Higgins launches into the non-Shavian: "This is what the English population calls an elementary education."

Consequently, when a written story is converted into a movie, it is useless to complain that the movie isn't true to the book. Of course it isn't. It couldn't be. You might as well complain that a stained glass representation of *Mona Lisa* didn't catch all the nuances of the painting, or for that matter that da Vinci didn't manage to catch the fire and gleam of stained glass.

In fact, if some moviemaker, anxious to lose his investment, were to make a movie that paralleled a printed story *precisely*, you probably wouldn't like it; for what is good on the printed page is not necessarily good in the screened image (and vice-versa).

This doesn't mean you can't make a bad movie from a good book. Of course you can, but that would be because the movie fails in its own terms, and not because it is untrue to the book. It is also possible for a movie to improve upon a book. *Oliver Twist* is not one of my favorites, but I am thoroughly delighted by the movie *Oliver*.

Why are books and movies so different? Books are a series of words. They are altogether language. Half a century ago and more, books were commonly illustrated and that added image, which in some cases (a notable example being *Alice in Wonderland*) vied with the printed word in importance. That has now disappeared and only the string of words remains. Therefore, for a book to be successful, that string of words must be well done, must catch the readers' minds and emotions. A bare string of words must substitute for image, sound, intonation, and everything else.

The movie, on the other hand, works very largely with image. Words exist in the form of dialogue; there are sound effects and musical accompaniment, but image is primary.

In some ways, the movie image is a much more subtle tool than the words in the book. An effect that can only be created by a paragraph of description can be caught in a moment when a fleeting expression is shown, or the gesture of a hand, or a sudden appearance of a knife or a clock—or almost anything.

And yet in other ways words are so pliable, so easy to bend into a flash of irony and wit, so successful in producing long satirical tirades, so subtle in revealing character.

Naturally, each art form to do its thing well must emphasize its strengths and slur over its weaknesses, and the result is two different stories—ideally, each wonderful.

There is a second difference between books and movies that is not artistic in origin, but economic. A movie is much more expensive to produce than a book.

For that reason, a book can make money if it sells as little as five thousand in hard cover, a hundred thousand in soft cover, and appears in a few foreign editions. Under such circumstances it will not make the author rich, but at least it will do enough to have the publisher smile and nod graciously if the writer suggests writing another book.

This means that the writer can aim to please fewer than one out of every thousand Americans. He can aim at a relatively small and specialized group and still make a living and gain success. (Thus, for many years I supported myself adequately by pleasing that small group of Americans who were science fiction readers.)

It further means that a writer can afford to be haughty. He can write a book that entirely pleases himself and that does not cater to the general public. He can write a difficult book, a puzzling book—whatever. After all, he need only be read by a fragment of the public to be successful. I don't say that writers scorn bestsellers as a matter of course; I merely say that they may do so if they wish.

Not so the moviemaker, who, if he is to get back his much larger investment, must seek an audience in the millions, perhaps even in the tens of millions. Failure to do so can mean the loss of a fortune. To please so many, the movie must be much more careful to hit some common denominator, and the temptation is always present to cheapen the story in consequence.

One common denominator is romance. A story can be written without romance and still do well. A movie without romance finds it much more difficult to be profitable. This means a young woman of improbable beauty is almost sure to find herself thrust into stories where she does not fit very well. . . .

Then, too, a movie is often made from a short story and, if a full-length feature is to be produced, much must be added—so that the screenwriter has all the more impetus to bring creativity of his own to the story. A good screenwriter can use this as an opportunity to improve the story greatly but, as in all other categories of endeavor, the number of good screenwriters is far fewer than the number of screenwriters. . . .

Stories [bought for films] are distinguished by the fact that some moviemaker saw in them something that might appeal to a far wider public than that for which they were originally designed. What's more, the moviemaker was willing to bet a great deal of money that his judgment was correct.

Usually, such judgments *are* correct. Even when the resulting movie fails, the fault is that of the movie-making and not of the merit of the underlying story.

. . . If you . . . have seen a movie inspired by [a story], please do not view the story as a version of the movie. Think of it as an entirely different production, written to the rhythm of a different artistic drum, for a different audience, and enjoy it on its own terms.

A more spirited view of words as superior to images is given in the following essay by Isaac.

The Ancient and the Ultimate

I once attended a seminar that dealt with communications and society. The role assigned to me was a small one, but I spent four full days there, so I had a chance to hear all the goings-on.

The very first night I heard a particularly good lecture by an extraordinarily intelligent and charming gentleman who was involved in the field of TV cassettes. He made out an attractive and, to my way of thinking, irrefutable case in favor of the cassettes as representing the communications wave of the future—or, anyway, one of the waves.

He pointed out that for the commercial programs intended to support the fearfully expensive TV stations and the frightfully avid advertisers, audiences in the tens of millions were an absolute necessity.

As we all know, the only things that have a chance of pleasing twenty-five to fifty million people are those that carefully avoid giving any occasion for offense. Anything that will add spice or flavor will offend someone and lose.

So it's the unflavored pap that survives, not because it pleases but because it gives no occasion for displeasing. (Well, some people—you and I, for instance—are displeased, but when advertising magnates add up the total number of you and me and others like us, the final sum sends them into fits of scornful laughter.)

Cassettes, however, that please specialized tastes are selling content only, and don't have to mask it with a spurious and costly polish or the presence of a high-priced entertainment star. Present a cassette on chess strategy with chessmen symbols moving on a chessboard, and nothing else is needed to sell X number of cassettes to X number of chess enthusiasts. If enough is charged per cassette to cover the expense of making the tape (plus an honest profit) and if the expected number of sales are made, then all is well. There may be unexpected flops, but there may be unexpected bestsellers, too.

In short, the television-cassette business will rather resemble the book-publishing business.

The speaker made this point perfectly clear, and when he said, "The manuscript of the future will not be a badly typed sheaf of papers but a neatly photographed sequence of images," I could not help but fidget.

Maybe the fidgeting made me conspicuous as I sat there in the front row, for the speaker then added, "And men like Isaac Asimov will find themselves outmoded and replaced."

Naturally I jumped—and everybody laughed cheerfully at the thought of my being outmoded and replaced.

Two days later, the speaker scheduled for that evening made a transatlantic call to say he was unavoidably detained in London, so the charming lady who was running the seminar came to me and asked me sweetly if I would fill in.

Naturally I said I hadn't prepared anything, and naturally she said that it was well known that I needed no preparation to give a terrific talk, and naturally I melted at the first sign of flattery, and naturally I got up that evening, and naturally I gave a terrific talk. (Well, everybody said so.) It was all very natural.

I can't possibly tell you exactly what I said because, like all my talks, it was off the cuff, but as I recall the essence was something like this:

The speaker of two days before having spoken of TV cassettes and having given a fascinating and quite brilliant picture of a future in which cassettes and satellites dominated the communications picture, I was now going to make use of my science-fiction expertise to look still further ahead and see how cassettes could be further improved and refined, and made still more sophisticated.

In the first place, the cassettes, as demonstrated by the speaker, needed a rather bulky and expensive piece of apparatus to decode the tape, to place images on a television screen, and to put the accompanying sound on a speaker.

Obviously, we would expect this auxiliary equipment to be made smaller, lighter, and more mobile. Ultimately we would expect it to disappear altogether and become part of the cassette itself.

Secondly, energy is required to convert the information contained in the cassette into image and sound, and this places a strain on the environment. (All use of energy does that, and while we can't avoid using energy, there is no value in using more than we must.)

Consequently we can expect the amount of energy required to translate the cassette to decrease. Ultimately we would expect it to approach a value of zero and disappear.

Therefore we can imagine a cassette that is completely mobile and self-contained. Though it requires energy in its formation, it requires no energy and no special equipment for its use thereafter. It needn't be plugged into the wall; it needs no battery replacements; it can be carried with you wherever you feel most comfortable about viewing it: in bed, in the bathroom, in a tree, in the attic.

A cassette as ordinarily viewed makes sounds, of course, and casts light. Naturally it should make itself plain to you in both image and sound, but for it to obtrude on the attention of others, who may not be interested, is a flaw. Ideally, the self-contained mobile cassette should be seen and heard only by you.

No matter how sophisticated the cassettes now on the market, or those visualized for the immediate future, they do require controls. There is an off-on knob or switch, and others to regulate color, volume, brightness, contrast, and all that sort of thing. In my vision, I want to make such controls operated, as far as possible, by the will.

I foresee a cassette in which the tape stops as soon as you remove your eye. It remains stopped till you bring your eye back, at which point it begins to move again immediately. I foresee a cassette that plays its tape quickly or slowly, forward or backward, by skips or with repetitions, entirely at will.

You'll have to admit that such a cassette would be a perfect futuristic dream: self-contained, mobile, non-energy-consuming, perfectly private, and largely under the control of the will.

Ah, but dreams are cheap, so let's get practical. Can such a cassette possibly exist? To this, my answer is: Yes, of course.

The next question is: How many years will we have to wait for such a deleriously perfect cassette?

I have that answer too, and quite a definite one. We will have it in minus five thousand years—because what I have been describing (as perhaps you have guessed) is the book!

Am I cheating? Does it seem to you that the book is *not* the ultimately refined cassette for it presents words only and no image, that words without images are somehow one-dimensional and divorced from reality, that we cannot expect to get information by words alone concerning a universe that exists in images?

Well, let's consider that. Is the image more important than the word?

Certainly if we consider man's purely physical activities, the sense of sight is by far the most important way in which he gathers information concerning the universe. Given my choice of running across rough country with my eyes blindfolded and my hearing sharp, or with my eyes open and my hearing out of action, I would certainly use my eyes. In fact, with my eyes closed I would move at all only with the greatest caution.

But at some early stage in man's development he invented speech. He learned how to modulate his expired breath and how to use different modulations of sound to serve as agreed-upon symbols of material objects and actions and—far more important—of abstractions.

Eventually he learned to encode modulated sounds into markings that could be seen by the eye and translated into the corresponding sound in the brain. A book, I need not tell you, is a device that contains what we might call "stored speech."

It is speech that represents the most fundamental distinction between man and all other animals (except possibly the dolphin, which may conceivably have speech but has never worked out a system for storing it).

Not only do speech and the potential capacity to store speech differentiate man from all other species of life who have lived now or in the past, but these capacities are something all men have in common. All known groups of human beings, however "primitive" they may be, can and do speak, and can and do have a language. Some "primitive" peoples have very complex and sophisticated languages, I understand.

What's more, all human beings who are even nearly normal in mentality learn to speak at an early age.

With speech the universal attribute of mankind, it becomes true that more information reaches us—as *social* animals—through speech than through images.

The comparison isn't even close. Speech and its stored forms (the written or printed word) are so overwhelmingly a source of the information we get that without them we are helpless.

To see what I mean, let's consider a television program, since that ordinarily involves both speech and image, and let's ask ourselves what happens if we do without one or the other.

Suppose you darken the picture and allow the sound to remain. Won't you still get a pretty good notion of what's going on? There may be spots rich in action and poor in sound that may leave you frustrated by dark silence, but if it were anticipated that you would not see the image, a few lines could be added and you would miss nothing.

Indeed, radio got by on sound alone. It used speech and "sound effects." This meant that there were occasional moments when the dialogue was artificial to make up for the lack of image: "There comes Harry now. Oh, he doesn't see the banana. Oh, he's stepping on the banana. There he goes." By and large, though, you could get along. I doubt that anyone listening to radio seriously missed the absence of image.

Back to the TV tube, however. Now turn off the sound and allow the vision to remain untouched—in perfect focus and full color. What do you get out of it? Very little. Not all the play of emotion on the face, not all the impassioned gestures, not all the tricks of the camera as it focuses here and there are going to give you more than the haziest notion of what is going on.

Corresponding to radio, which is only speech and miscellaneous sound, there were the silent movies, which were only images. In the absence of sound and speech, the actors in the silent films had to "emote." Oh, the flashing eyes; oh, the hands at the throat, in the air, raised to heaven; oh, the fingers pointing trustingly to heaven, firmly to the floor, angrily to the door; oh, the camera moving in to show the banana skin on the floor, the ace in the sleeve, the fly on the nose. And despite every extreme of inventiveness of visualization in its most exaggerated form, what did we have every fifteen seconds? An utter halt to the action while words flashed on the screen.

90

This is not to say that one cannot communicate after a fashion by vision alone—by the use of pictorial images. A clever pantomimist like Marcel Marceau or Charlie Chaplin or Red Skelton can do wonders—but the very reason we watch them and applaud is that they communicate so much with so poor a medium as pictorialization.

As a matter of fact, we amuse ourselves by playing charades and trying to have someone guess some simple phrase we "act out." It wouldn't be a successful game if it didn't require much ingenuity, and, even so, practitioners of the game work up sets of signals and devices that (whether they know it or not) take advantage of the mechanics of speech.

They divide words into syllables, they indicate whether a word is short or long, they use synonyms and "sounds like." In all of this, they are using visual images to *speak.* Without using any trick that involves any of the properties of speech, but simply by gesture and action alone, can you get across as simple a sentence as, "Yesterday the sunset was beautiful in rose and green"?

Of course a movie camera can photograph a beautiful sunset and you can point to that. This involves a great investment of technology, however, and I'm not sure that it will tell you that the sunset was like that *yesterday* (unless the film plays tricks with calendars—which represent a form of speech).

Or consider this: Shakespeare's plays were written to be acted. The image was the essence. To get the full flavor, you must see the actors and what they are doing. How much do you miss if you go to *Hamlet* and close your eyes and merely listen? How much do you miss if you plug your ears and merely look?

Having made clear my belief that a book, which consists

of words but no images, loses very little by its lack of images and has therefore every right to be considered an extremely sophisticated example of a television cassette, let me change my ground and use an even better argument.

Far from lacking the image, a book *does* have images— and, what's more, far better images, because personal, than any that can possibly be presented to you on television.

When you are reading an interesting book, are there no images in your mind? Do you not see all that is going on, in your mind's eye?

Those images are *yours.* They belong to you and to you alone, and they are infinitely better for you than those wished on you by others.

I saw Gene Kelly in *The Three Musketeers* once (the only version I ever saw that was reasonably faithful to the book). The sword fight between D'Artagnan, Athos, Porthos, and Aramis on one side and the five men of the Cardinal's Guard on the other, which occurs near the beginning of the picture, was absolutely beautiful. It was a dance, of course, and I reveled in it . . . But Gene Kelly, however talented a dancer he might be, does not happen to fit the picture of D'Artagnan that I have in my mind's eye, and I was unhappy all through the picture because it did violence to "my" *The Three Musketeers.*

This is not to say that sometimes an actor might not just happen to match your own vision. Sherlock Holmes in my mind just happens to be Basil Rathbone. In *your* mind, however, Sherlock Holmes might *not* be Basil Rathbone; he might be Dustin Hoffman, for all I know. Why should all our millions of Sherlock Holmes's have to be fitted into a single Basil Rathbone?

You see, then, why a movie or a television program, however excellent, can never give as much pleasure, be as absorbing, fill so important a niche in the life of the imagination, as a book can. To the television program we need only bring an empty mind and sit torpidly while the display of sound and image fills us, requiring nothing of our imagination. If others are watching, they are filled to the brim in precisely the same way, all of them, and with precisely the same-sounding images.

The book, on the other hand, demands cooperation from the reader. It insists that he take part in the process.

In doing so, it offers an interrelationship that is made to order by the reader himself for the reader himself—one that most neatly fits his own peculiarities and idiosyncrasies.

When you read a book you create your own images, you create the sound of various voices, you create gestures, expressions, emotions. You create *everything* but the bare words themselves. And if you take the slightest pleasure in creation, the book has given you something the television program can't.

Furthermore, if ten thousand people read the same book at the same time, each nevertheless creates his own images, his own sound of the voice, his own gestures, expressions, emotions. It will not be one book but ten thousand books. It will not be the product of the author alone, but the product of the interaction of the author and each of the readers separately.

What, then, can replace the book?

I admit that the book may undergo changes in non-essentials. It was once handwritten; it is now printed. The technology of publishing the printed book has advanced in a hundred ways, and in the future a book may be turned out electronically from a television set in your house.

In the end, though, you will be alone with the printed word, and what can replace it?

Is all this wishful thinking? Is it just that I make my living out of books, so I don't want to accept the fact that books may be replaced? Am I just inventing ingenious arguments to console myself?

Not at all. I am certain that books will not be replaced in the future, because they have not been replaced in the past.

To be sure, many more people watch television than read books, but that is not new. Books were *always* a minority activity. Relatively few people read books before the invention of television, and before radio, and before anything you care to name.

As I said, books are demanding and require creative activity on the part of the reader. Not everyone, in fact darned few, are ready to give what is demanded, so they don't read, and they won't read. They are not lost just because the book fails them somehow; they are lost by nature.

In fact, let me make the point that reading itself is difficult, inordinately difficult. It is not like talking, which every even halfway normal child learns without any program of conscious teaching. Imitation beginning at the age of one will do the trick.

Reading, on the other hand, must be carefully taught and, usually, without much luck.

The trouble is that we mislead ourselves by our own definition of literacy. We can teach almost anyone (if we try hard enough and long enough) to read traffic signs and to make out instructions and warnings on posters, and to puzzle out newspaper headlines. Provided the printed message is short and reasonably simple and the motivation to read it is great, almost everyone can read.

And if this is called literacy, then almost every American is literate. But if you then begin to wonder why so few Americans read books (the average American out of school, I understand, does not even read one complete book a year), you are being misled by your own use of the term "literate."

Few people who are literate in the sense of being able to read a sign that says NO SMOKING ever become so familiar with the printed word and so at ease with the process of quickly decoding by eye the small and complicated shapes that stand for modulated sounds that they are willing to tackle any extended reading task—as, for instance, making their way through one thousand consecutive words.

Nor do I think it's entirely a matter of the failure of our educational system (though heaven knows it's a failure). No one expects that if one teaches every child how to play baseball, they will all be talented baseball players, or that every child taught how to play the piano will be a talented pianist. We accept in almost every field of endeavor the notion of a talent that can be encouraged and developed but cannot be created from nothing.

Well, in my view, reading is a talent too. It is a very difficult activity. Let me tell you how I discovered that.

When I was a teenager, I sometimes read comic magazines, and my favorite character, if you're interested, was Scrooge McDuck. In those days comic magazines cost ten cents, but of course I read them for nothing off my father's newsstand. I used to wonder, though, how anyone would be so foolish as to pay ten cents, when by simply glancing through the magazine for two minutes at the newsstand he could read the whole thing.

Then one day on the subway to Columbia University, I found myself hanging from a strap in a crowded car with nothing handy to read. Fortunately the teenage girl seated in front of me was reading a comic magazine. Something is better than nothing, so I arranged myself so I could look down on the pages and read along with her. (Fortunately I can read upside down as easily as right side up.)

Then, after a few seconds I thought, Why doesn't she turn the page?

She did, eventually. It took minutes for her to finish each double-page spread, and as I watched her eyes going from one panel to the next and her lips carefully mumbling the words, I had a flash of insight.

What she was doing was what I would be doing if I were faced with English words written phonetically in the Hebrew, Greek, or Cyrillic alphabet. Knowing the respective alphabets dimly, I would have to first recognize each letter, then sound it, then put them together, then recognize the word. Then I would have to pass on to the next word and do the same. Then, when I had done several words this way, I would have to go back and try to get them in combination.

You can bet that under those circumstances I would do very little reading. The *only* reason I read is that when I look at a line of print I see it all as words, and at once.

And the difference between the reader and the non-reader grows steadily wider with the years. The more a reader reads, the more information he picks up, the larger his vocabulary grows, the more familiar various literary allusions become. It becomes steadily easier and more fun for him to read, while for the non-reader it becomes steadily harder and less worthwhile.

The result of this is that there are and *always have been*

(whatever the state of supposed literacy in a particular society) both readers and non-readers, with the former making up a tiny minority, of, I guess, less than one percent.

I have estimated that four hundred thousand Americans have read some of my books (out of a population of two hundred million), and I am considered, and consider myself, a successful writer. If a particular book should sell two million copies in all its American editions, it would be a remarkable bestseller—and all that would mean would be that 1 percent of the American population had managed to nerve themselves to buy it. Of that total, moreover, I'm willing to bet that at least half would manage to do no more than stumble through some of it in order to find the dirty parts.

Those people, those non-readers, those passive receptacles for entertainment, are terribly fickle. They will switch from one thing to another in the eternal search for some device that will give them as much as possible and ask of them as little as possible.

From minstrels to theatrical performances, from the theater to the movies, from the silents to the talkies, from black-and-white to color, from the record player to the radio and back, from the movies to television to color television to cassettes. . . .

What does it matter?

But through it all, the faithful less-than-1-percent minority stick to the books. Only the printed word can demand as much from them, only the printed word can force creativity out of them, only the printed word can tailor itself to their needs and desires, only the printed word can give them what nothing else can.

The book may be ancient but it is also the ultimate, and

readers will never be seduced away from it. They will remain a minority, but they will *remain.*

So despite what my friend said in his speech on cassettes, writers of books will never be outmoded and replaced. Writing books may be no way to get rich (oh, well, what's money?), but as a profession, it will always be there.

9

Bright Future: Writing Non-Fiction

[an article by I.A.]

You may have heard the statement: "One picture is worth a thousand words."

Don't you believe it. It may be true on occasion—as when someone is illiterate, or when you are trying to describe the physical appearance of a complex object. In other cases, the statement is nonsense.

Consider, for instance, Hamlet's great soliloquy that begins with "To be or not to be," the poetic consideration of the pros and cons of suicide. It is 260 words long. Can you get across the essence of Hamlet's thought in a quarter of a picture—or, for that matter, in 260 pictures? Of course not. The pictures may be dramatic illustrations of the soliloquy if you already know the words. The pictures by themselves, to someone who has never read or heard *Hamlet*, will mean nothing.

As soon as it becomes necessary to deal with emotions,

ideas, fancies—abstractions in general—only words will suit. The modulation of sound, in countless different ways, is the only device ever invented by human beings that can even begin to express the enormous complexity and versatility of human thought.

Nor is this likely to change in the future. You have heard that we live in an age of communication and you may assume, quite rightly, that amazing and fundamental changes are taking place in that connection. These changes, however, involve the *transmission* of information and not its nature. The information itself remains in the form it was in prehistoric times: speech, and the frozen symbology of speech that we call writing.

We can transmit information in sign language, by semaphore, by blinking lights, by Morse code, by telephone, by electronic devices, by laser beams, or by techniques yet unborn—and in every case, we are transmitting words.

There is the fundamental rule, then. In the beginning was the word (as the Gospel of St. John says in a different connection), and in the end will be the word. The word is immortal. And it follows from this that just as we had the writer as soon as writing was invented five thousand years ago, so we will have the writer, of necessity, for as long as civilization continues to exist. He may write with other tools and in different forms, but he will *write.*

Having come to the conclusion that writers have a future, we might fairly ask next: What will the role of the writer be in the future? Will writers grow less important, play a smaller role in society, or will they hold their own?

Neither.

It is quite certain that writers' skills will become steadily more important as the future progresses—providing, that is, that we do not destroy ourselves, and that there *is* a future of significance, one in which social structures continue to gain in complexity and in technological advance.

The reasons are not difficult to state.

To begin with, technological advance has existed as long as human beings have. Our hominid ancestors began to make and use tools of increasing complexity before the present-day hominid we call *Homo sapiens* had yet evolved. Society changed enormously as technology advanced. Think what it meant to human beings when agriculture was invented: herding . . . pottery . . . weaving . . . metallurgy. Then, in historic times, think of the changes introduced by gunpowder: the magnetic compass . . . printing . . . the steam engine . . . the airplane . . . television.

Technological change feeds on previous technological change, and the rate of change increases steadily. In ancient times, inventions came so infrequently and their spread was so slow that individual human beings could afford to ignore them. In one person's generation, nothing seemed to change as far as social structure and the quality of life was concerned. But as the rate of change increased, that became less true, and after 1800, the Industrial Revolution made it clear that life—everyday life—was changing rapidly from decade to decade and then from year to year and, by the closing portion of the twentieth century, almost from day to day. The gentle zephyr of change that our ancestors knew has become a hurricane.

We know that change is a confusing and unsettling matter. It is difficult for human beings to adjust to change. There is an automatic resistance to change, and that resistance diminishes the advantages we can obtain from change. From generation to generation, then, it has become more and more important to explain the essentials of change to the general public, making people aware of the benefits to be derived from change and of the dangers that they must beware of as a result. That has never been more important than it is now; and it will be steadily more important in the future.

We live in a time when advances in science and technology can solve the problems that beset us: increasing the food supply, placing reproductive potentialities under control, removing pollution, multiplying efficiency, obtaining new sources of energy and materials, defeating disease, expanding the human range into space, and so on.

Advances in science and technology also create problems to bedevil us: producing more dangerous weapons, creating more insidious forms of pollution, destroying the wilderness and disrupting the ecological balance of earth's living things.

At every moment, the politicians, the businesspeople, and to some extent every portion of the population must make decisions on both individual and public policy that will deal with matters of science and technology.

To choose the proper policies, to adopt this and reject that, one must know something about science and technology. This does not mean that everyone must be a scientist, as we can readily see from the analogy of professional sport and its audience. Millions of Americans watch with fascinated intentness games of baseball, football, basketball, and so on. Very few of them can play the game with any skill; very few know enough to be able to coach a team; but almost all of them know enough about the game to appreciate what is going on, to cheer and groan at appropriate times, and to feel all the excitement and thrills of the changing tides of fortune. That must be so, for without such understanding, watching a game is merely a matter of watching chaos.

And so it must be that as many people as possible must know enough about science and technology to be members of an intelligent *audience*, at least.

It will be the writer, using words (with the aid of illustrations where that can make the explanation simpler or raise the interest higher, but *primarily* using words), who will endeavor to translate the specialized vocabulary of science and technology into ordinary English.

No one suggests that writing about science will turn the entire world into an intelligent audience, that writers will mold the average person into a model of judgment and creative thought. It will be enough if they spread the knowledge as widely as possible; if some millions, who would otherwise be ignorant (or, worse, swayed by meaningless slogans), would, as a result, gain some understanding; if those whose opinions are most likely to be turned into action, such as the political and economic rulers of the world, are educated.

H.G. Wells said that history was a race between education and catastrophe, and it may be that the writer will add just sufficient impetus to education to enable it to outrace catastrophe. And if education wins by even the narrowest of margins, how much more can we ask for?

Nor is a world that is oriented more in the direction of science and technology needed merely for producing better judgments, decisions, and policies. The very existence of science and technology depends on a population that is both understanding and sympathetic.

There was a time when science and technology depended strictly on individual ideas, individual labor, and individual financial resources. We are terribly attracted to the outmoded stereotype of the inventor working in his home workshop, of the eccentric scientist working in his home laboratory, of the Universe of Ignorance being assaulted by devices built of scraps, string, and paste.

It is so no longer. The growing complexity of science and technology has outstripped the capacity of the individual. We now have research teams, international conferences, industrial laboratories, large universities. And all these resources are strained, too.

Increasingly, the only source from which modern science and technology can find sufficient support to carry on its work is from that hugest repository of negotiable wealth—the government. That means the collective pocketbook of the taxpayers of the nation.

There has never been a popular tax, or an unreluctant taxpayer, but some things will be paid for more readily than others. Taxpayers of any nation are usually ready to pay enormous sums for military expenses, since all governments are very good at rousing hatred and suspicion against foreigners.

But an efficient military machine depends, to a large extent, on advances in science and technology, as do other more constructive and less shameful aspects of society. If writers can be as effective in spreading the word about science and technology as governments are at sowing hatred and suspicion, public support for science is less likely to fail, and science is less likely to wither.

Moreover, science and technology cannot be carried on without a steady supply of scientists and engineers; an increasing supply as the years go on. Where will they come from?

They will come from the general population, of course. There are some people who gain an interest in science and technology in youth and can't be stopped, but they, by themselves, are simply not numerous enough to meet the needs of the present let alone the future. Many more youngsters would gain such an interest only if they were properly stimulated.

Again, it is the writer who might catch the imagination of young people, and plant a seed that will flower and come to fruition. Thus I have received a considerable number of letters from scientists and engineers in training who have taken the trouble to tell me that my books were what had turned them toward science and technology. I am quite convinced that other science writers get such letters in equal numbers.

Let me make two points, however.

First, in order to write about science, it is not entirely necessary to be deeply learned in every aspect of science (no one can be, these days) or even in some one aspect— although that helps. To know science well can make you a "science writer," but any intelligent person who has a good layperson's acquaintance with the scientific and technological scene can write a useful article on some subject related to science and technology. He can be a *writer* dealing with science.

Here is an example:

Digital clocks seem to be becoming ever more common these days and the old-fashioned clock dial seems to be fading away. Does that matter? Isn't a digital clock more advanced? Won't children be able to tell time at once, as soon as they can read, instead of having to decipher the dial?

Yet there are disadvantages to a possible disappearance of the dial that perhaps we ought to keep in mind.

There are two ways in which anything might turn—a key in a lock, a screw in a piece of wood, a horse going around a race track, Earth spinning on its axis. They are described as "clockwise" and "counterclockwise." The first is the direction in which the hands on a clock move; the second is the opposite direction. We are so accustomed to dials that we understand clockwise and counterclockwise at once and do not make a mistake.

If the dial disappears (and of course it may not, for fashion is unpredictable) clockwise and counterclockwise will become meaningless and there is no completely adequate substitute. If you clench your hands and point the thumbs upward, the fingers of the left hand curl clockwise and those of the right hand counterclockwise. You might substitute "left-hand twist" and "right-hand twist," but no one stares at clenched hands as intently and as often as at clock dials, and the new terms will never be as useful.

Again, in looking at the sky, or through a microscope, or at any view that lacks easily recognizable reference marks, it is common to locate something by the clock dial. "Look at that object at eleven o'clock," you may say—or five o'clock, or two o'clock, or whatever. Everyone knows the location of any number from one to twelve on the clock dial and can use such references easily.

If the dial disappears, there will again be no adequate substitute. You can use directions, to be sure—northeast, south by west, and so on, but no one knows the compass as well as the clock.

Then, too, digital clocks can be misleading. Time given as 5:50 may seem roughly five o'clock, but anyone looking at a dial will see that it is nearly six o'clock. Besides, digital clocks only go up to 5:59 and then move directly to 6:00, and youngsters may be confused as to what happened to 5:60 through 5:99. Dials give us no such trouble.

One can go on and find other useful qualities in dials versus digits, but I think the point is clear. An article can be written that has meaning as far as technology is concerned and will provoke thought and yet not require a specialist's knowledge. We can't all be science writers, but we can all be writers about science.

The second point to be made is that I do *not* say that writers won't be needed in increasing numbers in other fields.

As computers and robots take over more of the dull labor of humanity and leave human beings to involve themselves in more creative endeavors, education will have to change in such a way as to place increasing emphasis on creativity. No doubt, education by computer will become more and more important, and a new kind of writer—the writer of computer programs for education—will arise and become important.

Again, as leisure time continues to increase the world over, writing to fill that leisure time, in the form of books, plays, television or movie scripts, and so on, will be needed in greater numbers.

In other words, more and more writers of more and more different kinds will be needed as time goes on; but, of them all, it is writers about science for whom the need will grow most quickly.

10

Imagination: The Joys of Writing Fiction

Many fiction writers used to "make things up" in their heads when they were children, either for their own amusement or to entertain other children. Storytelling is an ancient art, possibly ingrained in a species equipped with an over-developed cerebral cortex trying to cope with reality the best it can. But not all humans grow up to be storytellers for others.

Perhaps you are, or you know, someone who can imagine such elaborate, structured, vivid fantasies that you wonder why anyone would bother writing them down in cold prose when by shutting the eyes you can see the whole thing in your head like a movie. Why bother when words will never convey the glorious inner reality? Why do people *write*?

Because writers write. Because the act of imagining is somehow completed when put into words and shared with others.

Dreams cannot be hoarded selfishly in the mind, lying piled one upon the other, getting dog-eared and faded, but must be generously spilt out into the world.

—ELIZABETH GOUDGE

The crucial thing for a writer is the ability to make up coherent worlds.

—PETER DICKINSON

. . . [S]uccessful fiction writing . . . depends on privacy, secrecy, and a writer's occasional ability to take himself by surprise.

—JOHN MORTIMER

For in art, life is present in all its immediate brilliance; it has been rescued from the twofold oblivion which threatens it, and yet it preserves intact the transitory substance of time. Through art, the narrator can rise above his own death.

—GERMAINE BREE ON PROUST

Don't forget, and don't let your reader forget, that the small world in which you have held him for the last hour or two hasn't ended. Be aware, and make him aware, that tomorrow all of its remaining inhabitants will pick up the broken fragments of their lives, and carry on.

—JOSEPH HANSEN

Much of what we see in the universe . . . starts out as imaginary. Often you must imagine something before you can come to terms with it.

—CLIFFORD D. SIMAK

Man consists of body, mind, and imagination. His body is faulty, his mind untrustworthy, but his imagination has made him remarkable. In some centuries, his imagination has made life on this planet an intense practice of all the lovelier energies.

—JOHN MASEFIELD

"OF COURSE IT'S FICTION. IF IT WAS NON FICTION, I'D HAVE ALL SORTS OF REFERENCE MATERIAL AND I WOULDN'T NEED YOU."

The imagination, like the intellect, has to be used, and a creative writer ought to exercise it all the time. There is no idea, however insignificant or vague it may be, that the imagination cannot touch to new beginnings, turning it around and around in different lights, playing with it, *listening* to it.

—B. J. CHUTE

Help us to have the sense to climb high places of memory and of imagination, so that we may remember the beauty that lies behind and believe in the beauty that lies before.

—PRAYER BY WALTER RUSSELL BOWIE

11

In Praise of Specialized Fiction

Some of the most popular fiction ever written is described as "specialized" or "genre"—it falls into a particular category and usually has its own dedicated readers, in contrast to "mainstream" fiction which deals with—well, what *does* it deal with? You'll have to ask someone else since we confess that we usually read specialized fiction. And write it.

It's wonderful stuff, we think. You head for that section in a bookstore and see what's been added lately. And come home financially poorer, but richer where it counts.

There are all sorts of specialized fiction—romances, gothics, thrillers, mysteries, sports stories, westerns, fantasy, science fiction, and others. What you read and what you write is, again, a matter of taste.

First we have a few words of praise about mysteries: The essential human dilemma is consciousness. This means awareness of change and, with it, various fears—of time passing, uncertainty, meaninglessness, dehumanization, abandonment, being unable to cope—but ah, isn't the worst the fear of death?

Death is, as the cliché has it, the final mystery. Solving mysteries (even in stories not involving murder) is a neat way of giving human beings a (temporarily) comfortable feeling of being in control, able to understand the very worst aspects of existence.

In a non-murder mystery, there is still a solution, giving the reader a sense of completion and closure, with purpose and meaning to life. In a murder mystery, learning the how and why of one death makes all death a little more understandable. Furthermore, if the murderer is caught, the reader is reassured that destructive elements (in the world and inside the person) can be discovered, understood, and stopped.

We are obviously partial to the more old-fashioned mystery, where deductive reasoning is at a premium and everything ends satisfactorily. We are not personally in favor of stories about explicit, senseless brutality and killing. Real life has plenty, but we don't believe that human nature is basically "primitive evil" covered by a thin veneer of civilization.

According to many authors (some with several degrees after their names), stripping off the veneer reveals a brute who gets pleasure from killing. Like animals? But animals don't do that. Carnivores kill to eat, not to hang heads on their living room walls. Animals of the same species fight over mates and territory, with rules and behavior to make it possible that no one will die.

Human beings are animals who are even more specialized for cooperation, not battle. Humans grow up human, live in groups, and form civilizations—all through cooperation.

Perhaps it's getting harder to cooperate, the more crowded the world is. We shudder reading about Calhoun's rats, whose behavior increased in abnormality and murderousness with overpopulation. Research has shown that the more people present when humans commit violence, the less likely anyone is to come to the rescue. World population increases by eighty million people per year. . . .

Well, it will probably be good for the mystery writers.

I suppose it's simply awful for a little old lady to go around bopping people off, so to speak, but I do so enjoy this type of writing.

—ELIZABETH DALY
[who started writing
mysteries at age 60]

I'm not a cynic, nor do I have Jane Marple's guilty-till-proven-innocent attitude, but like Jane, I don't accept surface appearances. Give me a murder in quiet, family surroundings, the kind you read about in the papers—not the explosive, gangster type.

—AGATHA CHRISTIE

[Agatha Christie's] sleight of hand is to reveal and render harmless the death and hostility that haunt us—no matter how hard we pretend they do not—by incorporating them into a game.

—RALPH TYLER

There is one more point to be made about mystery fiction. A great deal of it has been written by, and read by, women. All sorts of arguments have been promulgated to account for this, from the lack of female squeamishness about gore (due to monthly acquaintance with it) to the possibility that the feeble Y chromosome makes male humans more physically vulnerable. . . .

But we don't go along with these theories, although it is true that while Percy was falling and fainting on the thorns of life, Mary Shelley was writing Frankenstein. One must be charitable. Many men write good mystery stories.

[John McAleer about Rex Stout]: It was in these [Nero Wolfe] stories that his vision and his artistry came together in perfect harmony to express those views that were his contribution to the preservation of the social order and the dignity of the human condition.

And some men who write mysteries provoke their writing spouses into contemplating blunt instruments. [JANET] When Isaac writes science fiction, his face is set into what looks like a permanent frown, indicating that he is puzzling out the plot as he goes along (knowing the ending he's heading toward, of course). Sometimes his facial expression is so reminiscent of those encountered in emergency room patients that I run for my stethoscope, only to be told that I've interrupted his train of thought.

But when Isaac is writing mysteries, he is obnoxious. He smiles smugly and announces he's just thought of a clever mystery gimmick and will now write the story, easily, quickly, no doubt perfectly. He talks about how easy it is to think up mysteries. I think about my three boxes of rejected mystery manuscripts and refrain from wrapping my stethoscope around his neck. I go to my word processor and try to think up a mystery plot. Nothing happens, but in the other room a word processor is going one hundred words per minute.

I love him. I do not pull the plug.

[This is Isaac writing now.] Neither Janet nor I know most of the specialized fields of fiction from personal effort, though we suspect that to those who can write any one of them, they are a great deal of fun. We have both written mystery and science fiction, however; so, since Janet has written about mysteries, I will do a bit of writing about science fiction.

Janet has mentioned my blitheness when writing mysteries and my frowning misery when writing science fiction. There's a reason for it. I find science fiction a lot more difficult. It's not just that in science fiction it helps to understand science. You can bone up on that, and after all you frequently have to bone up on such things as poisons, wills, law courts, and so on for mysteries. It's something else. It's a matter of the background society.

In mysteries, once I have a gimmick and develop a plot about it, I'm home safe. The society I use is the one I live in and I have no trouble with it.

In science fiction, on the other hand, the plot works itself out against the background of a society different from our own; different, usually, as a result of some scientific or technological change. The society has not only to be different, it has to be interesting, self-consistent, and plausible.

Naturally, you cannot concentrate on a science fiction plot to the extent of obscuring the social background since, ideally, the plot wouldn't work *except* in that background. Neither can you describe the background so enthusiastically that the reader loses sight of the plot. Both must be interwoven, and it is that interweaving that represents the difficulty in good science fiction.

That is the reason it once took me only seven weeks to

write a full-length mystery, but it takes me seven to nine *months* to write a science fiction novel, months that include many sleepless nights, virtually all of them spent brooding on the society and virtually none of them involved with the plot.

It strikes me, though, that if science fiction is harder to write than other forms of fiction, it has greater rewards. Literature sometimes has the ability to change society as, most notably, in the popular reformist books of Charles Dickens. Such books are few, however, except in the field of science fiction. Science fiction deals with technological change, the one change that is most likely to produce permanent overall alterations (whether for better or for worse) in society. It can not only predict accurately sometimes, it can *influence*.

Both Jules Verne and H. G. Wells, for instance, wrote highly popular stories about trips to the moon in the nineteenth and early twentieth centuries. Well, scientists and engineers who began to deal with rocketry realistically in the 1920s had read science fiction. Men such as Robert Goddard and Werner von Braun had read H. G. Wells, for instance, and had been inspired by him. As for the space pioneer, Tsiolkovsky, he even tried his hand at science fiction himself.

This is not to say that science fiction taught them any rocketry. As a matter of fact, Wells used an anti-gravity device to get to the moon and Verne used a gigantic gun, and both of these devices can be dismissed out of hand as ways of reaching the moon.

Nevertheless, science fiction stirred the imagination, and launched most of the rocketeers on their vocations.

Even a nineteen-year-old lad can change the world. Let

me explain: Industrial robots are appearing on the assembly line with increasing frequency. These robots are rapidly being made more versatile, capable, and "intelligent." It isn't far-fetched to say that in a couple of decades this robotization will be seen to have changed the face of society permanently.

Is there anyone we can credit for this? Perhaps the one person who most nearly deserves it is Joseph F. Engelberger, who founded a firm devoted to the design and production of robots in the late 1950s and kept it going until the coming of the microchip in the 1970s made robot manufacture feasible. He then became the major robot producer in the world.

And how did Engelberger come to do this? Some years before, according to his own account, when he was still a college undergraduate, he became enthusiastic about the possibility of robots after reading a book named *I, Robot* written by Isaac Asimov.

I, Robot was a collection of nine stories written by me during the 1940s (the first was written in 1939, actually, when I was nineteen years old.) These were the first notable science fiction stories in which a robot was treated neither as nemesis nor as symbol, but was considered a machine with built-in safeguards—the Laws of Robotics. (In fact, the very word "robotics" was invented by me and was first used in print in one of the first of these stories.)

Just as many rocketeers received their initial inspiration from Wells, so did many early roboticists receive theirs from me.

It had not been my intention to change the world, you understand. I wrote my robot stories only to make a little money to pay my college tuition and to see my name in print. If I had been writing any other kind of fiction, that's all I would have gotten.

But I was writing science fiction—so I changed the world.

12

Writing Children's Books

"Children's Books" seems like a category to us, but "Books for Children" is a phrase that seems to demand taking literally. We don't believe that any writer writes stories, articles, or books just for children.

> . . . she did not write "down" to children, nor at, nor for them exactly. She really wrote for and about the child who had been herself.
>
> —Naomi Lewis on E. Nesbit

> But I am very sure of this: that no one can write a book which children will like unless he write it for himself first.
>
> —A. A. Milne

Writing children's books is more than fun; through the process you relive being a child, perhaps not the child you actually were but the child you would have liked to be, often a more important figure to the person you now are.

We can't imagine writing children's books without liking to read them. And reread them, still. Some don't hold up—we didn't like *The Water Babies* then, and can't abide it now—but others mean more as the years go by, particularly if we've learned something about the author's life in the meantime.

Perhaps fashions in children's books change markedly, yet with all the grim (not Grimm) delving into the nitty-gritty of tortured suburban existence or dangerous urban ghettos or invasions by alien monsters, children rise above this fare. Yes, they look at TV and movies, getting more of the same, but what do they *love*? ET makes it home safely at last. Spock comes back to life. The Muppets' funny adventures end in . . .

SUCCESS: Children are trying to grow and learn. That's their biological job and most of them not only do it well but love the process. It's idiotic to say that the fondest desire of every human being is to return to the quiet, calm darkness of the womb. In the first place, the uterus is not quiet—or the trick of imitating the mother's heartbeat by putting a loud ticking clock into a crying puppy's bed wouldn't work—and unless the mother is practically bovine, the environment is certainly not calm much of the time. Well, it *is* dark, but has anyone seen a baby that preferred to crawl toward darkness instead of light?

In the second place, humans don't want to return to the passivity of the womb. This was a notion invented by depressed psychoanalysts who thought they were their mother's Best—and only—Beloved. Humans get pleasure from using their abilities. Watch a baby trying to learn to walk. He not only tries over and over, but resents being helped when he stumbles and falls, smacking his own bottom hard. The baby wants to DO IT HIMSELF, chortling with glee at each successful step.

Children like to read about success, whether it's winning the hand of the best princess or prince, saving a life, helping people who need it, beating the other team in the game of the year, or discovering another universe.

There are many kinds of success, of course, some of them more subtle than others (this includes dying courageously, or even just writing a novel), but we feel that at the end of a children's book, the reader should feel good. (More of this in another chapter.)

We hasten to say that children's books are not namby-pamby, if they're any good. (Actually, we don't know; we've never been able to read any of that kind.) But we do like children's books that have a leavening of humor, especially about difficult situations.

Here's A. A. Milne on the problem of using seven-league boots:

[In an introduction] Your fairy godmother has given you a pair of seven-league boots, and you go to call on the Baron. Ten strides and you are there. So the romancers say—but *are you there?* Only if the Baron lives 210 miles away . . .

The introduction is to his "adult fairytale" *Once On a Time*, but the problem is not fully worked out in the body of the novel. In a short story called "A Matter-of-fact Fairy Tale," also written for adults, Milne does it:

Eleven miles the wrong side of the castle, Charming sat down to think it out. It was but two hours to sundown. Without his magic boots he would get to the castle too late. Of course, what he really wanted to do was to erect an isosceles triangle on a base of eleven miles, having two sides of twenty-one miles each. But this was before Euclid's time.

The best children's book writers are those who look at the world around them with a childlike vision—not childish,

which is an adult acting like a child, but with that innocent, open vision of the world that belongs to the various stages of growing up; a clearer, more immediate, more specific, more honest, less judging vision than the adult one.
—CHARLOTTE ZOLOTOW

Knowing what children want is never enough. You can't write about sports if you never really liked baseball, fishing, motorcycles, or whatever. The aficionado will know immediately that you are faking. Truth emerges from between the lines. No matter what the subject may be, every book is a self-portrait of the author.
—WINIFRED MADISON

. . . [A] children's book can be the perfect vehicle for an adult's most personal and private concerns.
—HUMPHREY CARPENTER

Children's knowledge of the world is often so small that they cannot judge, off-hand and without help, between the fantastic, the strange (that is rare or remote facts), the nonsensical, and the merely "grown-up" (that is ordinary things of their parents' world, much of which still remains unexplored). But they recognize the different classes, and may like all of them at times. Of course the borders between them are often fluctuating or confused; but that is not only true for children. We all know the differences in kind, but we are not always sure how to place anything that we hear.
—J. R. R. TOLKIEN

. . . Milne is reminding himself that the Secret Garden is always there for those who once knew it, and who can still find the door.
—HUMPHREY CARPENTER

People (including Carpenter) seem to believe that nowadays the ability to create "secret gardens" has been lost.

"WHERE HAVE YOU BEEN? PICTURE BOOKS
NOW DEAL WITH ALIENATION, ETHNICITY AND
THE CHANGING VIEW OF CONTEMPORARY SOCIETY."

We don't agree at all, regardless of the compelling argument that such fantasies were closely tied to the special world of the Victorian child. It's true that present-day children can turn on TV and tune into the adult world in a way that was never possible before, but they—and we—still love special secret places, even if they're in another galaxy, far, far away.

And children still like to make up stories. Perhaps some of the stories are used in computer games, and some are merely the choice between this or that "alternate ending" already written for a book, but imagination and the need to use it will never die.

Some children still feel about writing the way thirteen-year-old Emily of New Moon did, more than sixty years ago (undoubtedly speaking on behalf of her creator):

> " . . . [I]f you knew you would be poor as a church mouse all your life—if you knew you'd never have a line published—would you still go on writing—*would* you?" "Of course I would," said Emily disdainfully. "Why, I *have* to write—I can't help it by times—I've just *got* to."
>
> —L. M. MONTGOMERY

[From an I. A. essay "Writing for Young People"] I like to have the ideas in my novels sufficiently interesting and subtle to catch at the attention and thinking of intelligent adults, and, at the same time, to have the writing clear enough so as to raise no difficulties for the intelligent youngster. . . . It is good business. Attract an adult and you may well have someone who is here today and gone tomorrow. Attract a youngster and you have a faithful reader for life.

We think it's only right that A. A. Milne [in his *Autobiography*] should have the last word:

When We Were Very Young is not the work of a poet becoming playful, nor of a lover of children expressing his love, nor of a prose-writer knocking together a few jingles for the little ones, it is the work of a light-verse writer taking his job seriously even though he is taking it into the nursery. It seems that the nursery, more than any other room in the house, likes to be approached seriously.

13

In Celebration of Humor

Many writers write as if life were unrelievedly unpleasant if not absolutely tragic. Real life, however, persists in being full of humor and wisdom.

Notice the word order. To insure wisdom, work on having humor. Fortunately life is full of funny things, so it's easy to lubricate your sense of humor and go on to wisdom.

Twain, Dickens, and Wodehouse make you laugh at the eccentricities of humanity. In the process you find that you can recognize and accept human foibles in yourself, which makes life much simpler for all concerned. Never begrudge yourself, or your readers, a good laugh.

Laughter is genuinely good medicine—massaging the organs, improving the immune capacity, releasing salubrious brain hormones, and calming down the more primitive parts of the nervous system. You relax as you come to terms with the comic aspects of the universe and yourself, especially the absurdity of expecting things to be neat, predictable, and permanent.

If each of us is a way the universe becomes more aware of itself, then being alive is a big responsibility. To prevent it from being a burden, try laughing—and sharing the laughter with others by writing things they laugh at too. And don't confuse real laughter with what's generated by some modern fiction—a baring of the teeth in snarling defense.

Inevitably, there is a percentage of the population who cannot take their focus off the seriousness of any event. To tell the tragic or dramatic event wittily to these people is not to enhance an understanding or acceptance of the event, but to demean it. They love to pick their scabs. To these people I say, "Never be more than a city block from your psychiatrist. You haven't the sophistication to survive on your own."

—GREGORY MCDONALD

I don't think comedy is an escape from tragedy. They are both *life*.

—MIKE NICHOLS

Humor may be defined as the kindly contemplation of the incongruities of life, and the artistic expression thereof. . . . The essence of humor is human kindliness.

—STEPHEN LEACOCK

[I.A., in the introduction to our anthology "Laughing Space"] If we all laughed more, perhaps the world would get better. While laboring with heart and soul to correct the injustice, the misery, and the physical suffering of millions, why should we not also find occasion for laughter when possible? Is not part of the injustice and suffering the result of frowns and scowls that close the heart against the appeals of compassion and brotherhood, and might not fun and merriment let them in?

129

I've spent my whole life laughing.

—ROBYN ASIMOV

If you're not allowed to laugh in heaven, I don't want to go there.

—attributed to MARTIN LUTHER

Perhaps Mark Twain should have the last word on humor. Notice that he has Satan say it (in *The Mysterious Stranger*):

. . . For your race, in its poverty, has unquestionably one really effective weapon—laughter. Power, money, persuasion, supplication, persecution—these can lift at a colossal humbug—push it a little—weaken it a little, century by century; but only laughter can blow it to rags and atoms at a blast. Against the assault of laughter nothing can stand.

14

Writing—Forever?

Maybe not, but certainly as long as you can.

Wodehouse wrote—and wrote well—up to the day before he died at the age of ninety-three.

If you keep using your mind, you'll be more likely to keep it young, alert, sane, and creative. Growing older doesn't necessarily mean becoming senile, because if some cerebral neurons die off, others grow, especially the connections.

Have you noticed how everything you read and hear seems to be connected to all sorts of things in your head, and that those connections generate interesting ideas? The more you live, the more stuff is packed into your head, making life not only more interesting but possibly more creative. Just keep saying to yourself that those little brain cells of yours, however ancient they're getting, can and do develop more and more fascinating connections. . . .

As we said earlier, have faith—this time in your brain. It is not wearing out, just getting better.

And say that, loudly, when you forget appointments or to take the clothes out of the dryer or to start cooking dinner. Notice that such forgetfulness is at its peak when you are thoroughly absorbed in the words popping up on your monitor and say to yourself, "I'm not getting senile, dammit. I'm a *writer*!"

Starting at age seventy-six, Grandma Moses painted every day until her one hundred and first birthday. Did you write something today besides a shopping list? *Carpe diem*!

The idea that your brain runs down and becomes less receptive to new ideas is a myth. Learning capacities do not diminish with age. They are impaired only by disease or injury. You can always learn something new—or acquire new skills. . . . Where there is hope there is the potential for effort. Hope and effort both mean looking forward. And looking forward is an attribute of youth.

—HUGH DOWNS

Don't look back. Somethin' might be gaining on you.

—SATCHEL PAIGE

What saves me from the slough of despond and keeps me going is a delight in the senses, all five of them, and first and most compelling of all, an undying (so far) curiosity.

—LOUIS UNTERMEYER

I look back on my life like a good day's work; it was done and I feel satisfied with it. I was happy and contented, I knew nothing better and made the best out of what life offered. And life is what we make it, always has been, always will be.

—GRANDMA MOSES

. . . [G]rowing young into what others call "old age" is an achievement, a work of art. . . . Age, as someone has said, is where you're at in your head, an attitude of mind. . . . There exists no barrier in the later years to continued productivity and the enjoyment of new experiences, to creativity.

—ASHLEY MONTAGUE

. . . [Y]ou can't ever just sit back and let things happen.

Never give in. . . . Never, never think about your age, and keep occupied until the end.

—MARY MARTIN

Don't put important things off. Not only is life too short for us to realize our own potentialities for loving, but one isn't really "in" life if the important things are not said and done.

—EDWARD S. TAUBER

. . . [I]t was precisely when the thought of death had become a matter of indifference to me that I was beginning once more to fear death—under another form, it is true, as a threat not to myself but to my book, since for my book's incubation this life that so many dangers threatened was for a while at least indispensible.

—MARCEL PROUST

Without fear, there is no courage.

—JEFFREY SMITH

Worry in an empty context means that men die daily little deaths. But good anxiety—not about the things that were left undone long ago that return to haunt and harry men's minds, but active, vivid anxiety about what must be done and that quickly—binds men to life with an intense concern.

—MARGARET MEAD

To regret is to lose all over again. One ought, on the contrary, to give the happy days one has lived every possible chance of retaining their radiance and acquiring a second reality.

—MAURICE GOUDEKET

One must make a success of life, you know. That's one's first duty. I don't mean worldly success; I mean—being happy.

—ELIZABETH GOUDGE

If you will accept the results of the experience of an old man who has had a very chequered existence . . . there is nothing of permanent value (putting aside a few human affections), nothing that satisfies quiet reflection—except the sense of having worked according to one's capacity and light, to make things clear and to get rid of cant and shams of all sorts.

—THOMAS H. HUXLEY

Work is the means through which a writer puts into communicable and evocative and perhaps memorable form what he wants to say . . . and sometimes work is more than a satisfaction, a comfort, a habit, or a sanctuary. It is a joy. . . . Hundreds of writers, ancient and modern, have testified that a day without work is a day lost, and some of the saddest people in the long history of mankind have been creators whose creativity wore out before they did.

—WALLACE STEGNER

Do you think you're worn out? Please remember Frasier, the circus lion so old and handicapped that he was due for euthanasia until the chief warden of Lion Country Safari in California introduced him to a pride of eleven lionesses who had beaten up all the young males given to them as potential mates. Frasier evidently still had what it takes, for the lionesses brought him his food, held him up when he had difficulty walking, and bore his cubs.

This is eternity now; you are sunk as deep in it, wrapped as close in it, as you ever will be. The future is an illusion; it never arrives; it flies before you as you advance. Always it is today—and after death and a thousand years it is today. You have great deeds to perform and you must do them now.

—CHARLES FERGUSON

134

And when it's all over, perhaps someone will say thanks to you for having existed, and for having written. As a matter of fact, if even one reader liked just one thing you wrote, then you've been thanked.

The best "thank-you" we've ever read:

That was perhaps his central gift: Merrill Moore had energy. He had energy in quantities unknown to most men. And now that energy is still. Goodbye, Merrill. Back to the Universe. And thanks.

—JOHN CIARDI

Goodbye to you, too, John. And many thanks.

15

Other Writers

This is Isaac writing this chapter. Largely, this is Janet's book, you see. It was her concept and her drive that put it together. Even though much of it consists of quotations (and, to a great degree, of quotations from my essays and letters), it was Janet who chose the quotations and decided where to put them.

Just the same, since my name is on the book as coauthor, she insisted that I was not to be allowed to get away with the easy task of permitting myself to be quoted. She told me, quite firmly, that I would have to do some active writing.

Well, that's all right. I don't mind writing. I like it, in fact. So this section and the next have been assigned to me. I don't really know why, but "Yes, dear," seems to come naturally to me, since Janet is a very lovable person.

A writer is bound to meet other writers. Though a writer may be isolated in a small town, or in a rustic area, there are inevitable encounters. Even the isolated writer will travel to some large writing center (New York, Los Angeles, Boston) to visit a publisher or editor or agent, and one can scarcely do that without the likelihood of meeting other writers. (Once, when I was visiting Crown Publishers, I was introduced to Jean Auel, who was visiting them independently. Naturally, we each praised the other extravagantly and found the exercise refreshing. At least, I did.)

Then, too, there are conventions to attend, professional organizations to join, correspondences to strike up.

Whatever the means by which contact is initially made, it tends to be strongly maintained. There is comfort to be gained in interacting with other writers.

After all, writing is a one-person job; it's you and your pad or typewriter or word processor, and outsiders are not welcome. In fact, nonwriters haven't the faintest notion as to what is going on. Even those nonwriting people who are close to you, who may be friends or even relatives, don't seem to understand. There is a tendency, for instance, to suppose that when you are seated in your chair, sunk in silence, and gazing at nothing, you are obviously not working and therefore may safely be interrupted.

Other writers, however, share your problems and therefore understand them. There is the delight of sharing horror tales concerning publishers—of being able to complain of impercipient editors, of tone-deaf copy editors, of illiterate printers, of artists who refuse to read plain descriptions—to people who will be fully sympathetic. It is pleasant to talk of the outrageous rejections you have received, of the foolish letters from readers, of the requests for ridiculous revisions, and so on. Any writer, *any* writer, can talk endlessly (even when quite sober) about such things, and it warms the cockles of one's heart to know that others share your sufferings, and that you are not alone in a cruel world. You work off the internal tensions and pressures—lance the boil, so to speak—by pouring them into an understanding ear and you can then return to your work with increased pleasure.

Of course, it is conceivable that some writers might be

able to talk of six-figure advances, of fawning editors, of writing that seems to flow with perfect precision out of one's mind, and so on, but I don't think this would be wise. It would perform no therapeutic function, and such items would surely not be appreciated by most writers.

Perhaps there is a general impression that when writers meet they sit down to a cozy chat concerning the details of whatever it is they are now writing. Plots, the innocent may imagine, are swapped back and forth, and each writer gives his pal and colleague helpful hints on how to handle this knotty problem or how best to construct that particular bit of characterization.

I won't say this has never happened, but in nearly half a century of encountering hundreds of writers, I can tell you it has never happened to me. No writer has offered me details of his current work and I have certainly never had the slightest tendency to expose my work to him.

Why is this? There might just possibly be an element of superstition about it. There might be the feeling that any discussion of any job of writing, before it is finished, will jinx the whole thing. My own is a more rational view. My feeling is that if you blow off steam in *talking* about what you are writing, you reduce the impulse to *write* about it and the thing fades in your hands.

Is it possible that a writer feels that if he gives details concerning what he is doing, the other writer will steal it? It doesn't seem likely, actually, but if a fellow writer hears something it may stick in his mind and then find its way into his writing without his remembering when and where he heard it. He might honestly believe he had made it up— so why take chances?

When I was quite a beginner, I heard L. Sprague de Camp say solemnly, "Any portion of your work that you discuss before it is published enters the public domain and may be used by anyone." Whether that's so or not, I don't know—but again, why take chances?

Then too, why expose yourself to criticism? An editor who was also a writer once asked me to read a story of his and comment on it. He said, "I want you to be perfectly honest. If you don't like it, say so fearlessly, even if it means I never buy a story of yours again."

He thought he was joking, but I so strongly suspected he was not that I was unable to be "perfectly honest" about it.

Certainly *I* don't welcome criticism from any fellow writer, however qualified he might be to offer such comments. Nor do I make much distinction between "constructive criticism" and any other kind. I find no criticism to be constructive. (David Frost once said, "What a writer thinks of as constructive criticism is six thousand words of closely reasoned adulation.")

Nor is there any use in having any writer say, "No, I think you stumbled at this point. What you should really have your character do is thus-and-so."

After all, my mind works in a certain way, and other minds work in other ways. I don't say that my mind-working is better, but it *is* mine. Another's suggestion just doesn't fit my way of thinking.

Naturally, I must listen to editors and I must even sometimes follow their suggestions. That is a part of the writer's life and must be endured stoically, but it would be ridiculous actually to invite criticism from someone who is not your editor when you can just as easily refrain from breathing a word about what you're doing.

What do I say, then, when somebody says to me, "And what are you working on now?"

"WE COLLABORATE. I WRITE ABOUT THE MEN, MARGE WRITES ABOUT THE WOMEN, AND WALLY, A LANDSCAPE PAINTER, WRITES ABOUT THE SCENERY."

The proper answer is, "A novel." Period. Silence.

The closest interaction between writers takes place when they collaborate on a piece of work, but collaboration has always scared me. In my early days I sometimes collaborated on a work of fiction, or for that matter on a work of nonfiction, and I never found it pleasant. I was bound to disagree with my collaborator sooner or later, and whether I had my way, or he had his, or he and I ended in a compromise, there were wounds and hurt feelings.

I came to the conclusion that it is as disastrous (with rare exceptions) to plunge into a hasty collaboration as it is to enter into a hasty marriage. There *are* successful collaborations, though, and even I have had them.

This is, for instance, my seventh collaboration with Janet. To begin with, we love each other. In addition, in every case I allow her to do as much of the book as she can without my interfering in any way. Once she is completely done, I go over it, making some corrections and revisions, or even (at her request, as in this case) additions.

I do my best to make no changes for frivolous reasons, but only those which I am convinced are absolutely necessary. Even so, there are occasional times when we have words over some of the changes, and we have to keep a tight hold on our strong mutual affection to keep the discussions from ever reaching a wounding intensity.

Again, I have collaborated with Martin H. Greenberg on scores of anthologies. To begin with, however, editing an anthology is not as intimate an act as writing a book, and disagreements are not likely to run as deep. Secondly, Marty and I have mind-sets that are strongly similar. We've never had a serious disagreement.

So it *can* be done; but not easily, I warn you, not easily.

16

Integrity [I.A.]

"Integrity" is, to me, a somewhat stronger word than "honesty." "Honesty" often implies truth-telling and little more, but "integrity" implies wholeness, soundness, a complex philosophy of life.

To have integrity is to stand by your word, to have a sense of honor, to do what you have agreed to do and to do it as best you can. To have integrity is to be satisfied with nothing less than the best job you can do.

In that sense, anyone can have integrity, regardless of how small and unimportant a role he may play in the world, so it is certainly not unreasonable to expect a writer to have it.

To take a very simple case, a writer should not copy another's words and claim the credit for it. That's called "plagiarism," a word which is derived from a Latin word meaning "kidnapper"—for, after all, a plagiarist steals a writer's mental children.

Two stories may share very similar ideas and that may not necessarily be plagiarism, since ideas may well crop up independently in the minds of various authors. Besides, broadening the scope of the term may taint everything. It would be very hard to write a story of revenge without seeming to owe something to *Rigoletto* or to *The Count of Monte Cristo* or to *Hamlet*.

It is unlikely, however, that the *exact words* of several paragraphs in one story would appear in another without deliberate intent. Professional writers are not likely to fall prey to that crime (for that's what it is—it is not a peccadillo) if only because it is so easy to spot.

However, on two different occasions that I know of, a story of mine was copied over—word for word, from beginning to end—by young students and handed in as a school assignment under their own names. In one case, the teacher thought she recognized the story and consulted me in the matter. But in the other, the teacher was simple enough to think a student could duplicate, first time, the skills developed by a reasonably talented writer after decades of effort—and it was printed in a class magazine. Such student plagiarism may conceivably have happened many additional times without coming to my attention, and I'm sure every other writer with a considerable body of work must suffer in the same way.

There are, however, more subtle temptations than plagiarism, and these may be difficult to withstand. For instance, I am sometimes asked for a story or an essay, and a sum of money is offered. Sometimes the sum offered is quite below my usual fee, and I politely refuse the assignment. I don't always, though. Either because the task strikes me as particularly interesting, or because it is in a good cause, or because I am obliging a personal friend, I will undertake a job at a small fraction of what I would like to be paid.

Is it conceivable, however, that I would then say to myself that since I was only getting a tenth of my usual payment, I would dash off something carelessly on the grounds that a tenth of the money should get only a tenth of my effort? No, it is *not* conceivable. Once engaged, whatever the financial arrangements, I do the best I can.

Partly I like to think the reason is because I have integrity, but it is perfectly easy to place the thing on a selfish basis, too. After all, my return for my writing lies not only in the money I earn but in the opinions I gather. People think I am a good writer and expect good writing from me. If I am content to turn out a bad job, I will disappoint reader expectations and cause them to change their mind about my ability, and my earning capacity would dwindle. And even if readers were foolish enough to think bad writing was good just because my name was on it, *I* would know otherwise and I would be ashamed—and I have never been able to bear shame easily.

Integrity not only simplifies your life by making it easy to come to a decision, but it may keep you out of trouble.

A writer I knew slightly once suggested that I write a book very quickly and that I then engage in complicated financial dealings that would involve my risking some money to begin with. The book I wrote would, however, fail and that would enable me to write off so much money as a loss that I would save on taxes many, many times what I had invested in the book. Of course, we would have to be certain that my book would be a failure, so I would have to undertake to write a really bad one. I would be taking advantage of a "tax shelter" in this way, and it was all perfectly legal.

I shook my head. "No," I said. "It's perfectly possible for me to write a bad book while I am trying honestly to write a good one, but writing a bad one *on purpose* is more than I can undertake to do, no matter how much money it would save me on taxes and no matter how legal it might be."

145

I walked away and when, a couple of years later, I read that the fellow who had advanced this proposition to me was now on trial for this same "tax shelter," I was rather relieved that I had been simpleminded enough to have integrity.

Ah, well, but I make enough money not to be easily lured by the promise of a bit more money. I can afford to do what I want to do. What about writers who aren't so lucky, who have rent to pay, or a mortgage to deal with, or children to support? They *need* the money.

Consequently, when it seems that it is possible to make a lot of money by putting in a lot of steamy sex, or a heavy proportion of violence, or dialogue filled with gutter language, why not do it?

Well, why not, if you really want to do it, if it happens to be your thing? It is perfectly possible to write great literature, to illuminate the human condition, to move people to their depths, by writing stories that involve sex, violence, and vulgarity. After all, we all know that real life is full of sex, violence, vulgarity, and many other things that are reprehensible, if not disgusting. Is it not the job of the writer to portray these things and use them to give his reader a rounded knowledge of humanity?

Certainly, but what if it is *not* your thing? What if you're not even very good at it, but you know that many people would rather buy junk if it's sensational enough than good stuff that lacks sensation? Why not write junk and make money rather than write good stuff and starve?

I have no good answer for that. I'm not going to suggest that you starve. Since I have never gone hungry or known severe economic insecurity, it would ill become me to adopt a high, moral tone at the expense of someone who has.

However . . .

This is not a book intended to deal with the wealth and fame to be derived from writing. We would not attempt to write such a book, for we know full well that very few people who write, even those who are successful enough to publish, achieve wealth and fame. What's more, we don't know any secret (other than being born with a great deal of talent, drive, and perhaps a little luck) we can tell our readers that will enable them to become one of those few.

This book is intended to deal with the *joy* of writing, and we are certain that you can only have joy in writing if you write what you want to write, even though what you write does not make you a success.

If you must write what you don't want and don't like in order to make money, then there is a chance (not a certainty) that you will make money, but it *is* a certainty (or so it seems to me) that you will have little joy of it. Writing, then, will just be a distasteful job that you do because you must eat.

In that case, it might be better to find another job altogether (if you can) that will earn a living for you, and write as you please in your spare time. You will then at least have joy in your spare time and, who knows, perhaps writing what you like will someday bring you at least a little fame and money.

But the joy of it is best.

Unblemished let me live or die unknown; Oh, grant an honest fame, or grant me none!

—Alexander Pope

17

A Last Plea: Write What Makes People Feel Better

You don't have to be a head-in-the-sand optimist to write something that makes people feel better. Sad stories and great tragedies give emotional catharsis as well as food for thought.

But there's so much written that makes people feel worse, much worse, if not utterly hopeless and helpless. Readers are pushed to wallow in misery, convinced that it and only it is real—the brutality, the defeatism, the unpleasant, and the repulsive.

> Undeniably, there are many aspects of life and of existence and of the historical situation which are genuinely depressing, but we are under no obligation to be paralyzed by them. The problem of evil has a forgotten twin—the problem of good. . . . We are surely free to focus on the hopeful and the possible rather than the hopeless and the impossible.
> —JOSEPH GALLAGHER

So many writers seem to believe their special job is to shock the world by hitting it over the head with its own ugliness, forgetting that humanity has come a long way from the days of Victorian niceties and repression. No one puts skirts on piano legs any more. Furthermore, humans are well acquainted not only with their own psychological ugliness but with every horrible happening anywhere on the planet.

It certainly saves work, the hard work of constructive thinking, if you dispose of all loose ends by carefully thinking the worst. You can even go a step further, into the "Armageddon mentality," a fixed belief in final answers achieved at the cost of universal destruction (with salvation for those whose beliefs were properly fixed).

Writers should not try to exploit and augment the human tendency to "fall into helplessness" and its sequelae—apathy and negativity ("what's the use?"), wishful thinking, and violence. (I.A.—"Violence is the last refuge of the incompetent.")

It's all too easy to write about fear, trembling, and "sickness unto death" these days, when everyone now lives with the possibility of human-induced final destruction of our planet. It's much harder work to show that humans are more than their own pathology; that they are capable of noble effort.

If Love and Honor and Duty can be salvaged, then someone must write about them in a fashion which carries conviction. If we are to get along without them, then someone must describe a world from which they are absent in a fashion which makes that world seem worth having. And it is just the failure to do either of these things quite adequately which reveals the weakness of contemporary literature.

—Joseph Wood Krutch

It's simple for writers to excuse themselves by saying that everyone has to wallow in the slough of despond these days, and besides, sometimes it makes money. Or to claim that no matter how awful things were in Shakespeare's time (especially no antibiotics), the Elizabethans had standards to give them a sense of order, justice, and goodness—and that to the modern world these are only outmoded words.

There is no permanent TRUTH to cling to? But are not human beings intelligent creatures, with the responsibility for evolving truths, for living by them and writing about them?

> The writer is a creator of options. The writer enables people to discover new truths and new possibilities within themselves and to fashion new connections to human experience.
>
> —NORMAN COUSINS

> Books as well as food nourish and warm people. Books make connections.
>
> —MAY SARTON

> If you would not be forgotten as soon as you are dead, either write things worth reading or do things worth writing.
>
> —BENJAMIN FRANKLIN

> There is a place for satire—there are gangrenes that can only be burned out—but leave the burning to the great geniuses. It's better to heal than hurt.
>
> —L. M. MONTGOMERY

Meditation for Writers
(USEFUL IN PREVENTING IDENTITY CRISES AND EXISTENTIAL MALAISE)

I know who I am. I'm a member of the animal kingdom, phylum chordata, subphylum vertebrata, class mammalia, order primate—closely related to chimpanzees and gorillas, with whom we can now talk.

I'm of the family Homididae, genus homo, species homo sapiens sapiens. I'll try not to forget that we named ourselves (doubly) sapiens, the most intelligent species. Nobody else calls us that.

And I know where I am—on the third planet of a solar system in the Milky Way galaxy in a huge universe. Intelligent beings may be one of the ways this universe becomes conscious of itself and able to create beauty and meaning.

I am a living part of the universe but apart, because I'm self-aware. I share this aloneness with all human beings, isolated within the three pounds of gray brain inside our skulls.

But we can communicate.

And I will do the best I can.

The Writer's Working Library for Aid and Comfort

Anything that's an aid is also a comfort. It's best to find books that are useful to you, and that's an individual matter. Those listed below are books essential to the Asimovs.

Dictionaries: Webster's Second, Biographical, Geographical.

Encyclopedias Britannica and Americana.

Bartlett's Familiar Quotations.

The Harper Dictionary of Contemporary Usage.

World Almanac.

London Times Atlas.

Guinness Book of World Records.

Rhyming dictionary.

The Synonym Finder. (Janet's is well-worn. Isaac says he doesn't need one: "I have a large vocabulary, keep my style simple and my writing accessible.")

The Home Book of Verse.

Books of Names. (Janet uses books of babies' names; Isaac uses Webster's Biographical Dictionary for interesting last names in all languages, and in the back there's a list of first names.)

Wodehouse on names: "Odd how important story names are. It always takes me about as long to get them to my satisfaction as it does to write the novel."

And George Selden: "There's a mystery in names, something very important—and especially the names of living things: names make things be themselves."

We have a small list of books we've used in order to write better. Others have longer lists with important books you should know, but these are our favorites:

The Elements of Style, by Strunk and White.
Strictly Speaking and *A Civil Tongue,* by Edwin Newman.
An Almanac of Words at Play, by Willard R. Espy.

You should also have one or more of the many technical books on writing, especially if you don't already know about constructing stories and novels and articles, or how to type manuscripts and handle the business aspects. Look over all the books and find one of use to you.

We also have a list of BELOVED BOOKS, REREAD FREQUENTLY, for comfort, entertainment, and exposure to good writing.

The operative words are "REREAD FREQUENTLY." We love many books, but don't necessarily read them over and over.

All of Wodehouse, Twain, and Dickens (Isaac's choices for the best writers of all time).

All of Agatha Christie (for unadorned style and master story-telling).

Histories by Bruce Catton, Will and Ariel Durant.

Cervantes (Isaac has read *Don Quixote* in many translations).

Homer (ditto).

Ellis Peters's medieval mysteries.

Rosemary Sutcliffe's historical novels.

Charles Schulz's "Peanuts" books.

All of E. Nesbit, especially *The Enchanted Castle* and the three "Five Children" books.

All of Tolkien (Isaac has read *The Lord of the Rings* five times).

And, of course, Shakespeare.

AN EVEN MORE PERSONAL LIST (from Janet):

All of Gerald Durrell's books.

All of Clifford Simak's books, especially *City* and *A Choice of Gods*

All of Ruth Plumly Thompson's "Oz" books (now in paperback, thanks to the late Judy-Lynn Del Rey).

Zen Art for Meditation, by Stewart W. Holmes and Chimyo Horioka (Tuttle). A gem of wisdom and humor.

The Pocket Book of Verse, edited by M.E. Speare. My 1945 edition has been to college, to Europe several times with various people, and its end papers urge buying war bonds, but the paper is so good the inside of the book is in great physical shape. The selection is familiar and soothing.

The three "Emily" novels by L.M. Montgomery. About a writer.

All of the mysteries of Michael Innes, Rex Stout, and Josephine Tey. And many others.

Most of Frances Hodgson Burnett, especially *The Lost Prince*, which taught me at the age of eleven that mental discipline was desirable and possible.

The Joyous Story of Astrid, by L. Adams Beck. Read in childhood and many times since, it started an interest in Oriental philosophy.

Bel Ria and *The Incredible Journey,* by Sheila Burnford. Animal books that lift the spirit.

The Kingdom of the Winding Road, by Cornelia Meigs. I read it in the New Rochelle library when I was a small child, but never found a copy to buy until I was an intern in Philadelphia and haunted the now defunct Leary's Bookshop as a way of staying sane.

The Dog Who Wouldn't Be, by Farley Mowatt. One of the funniest, and saddest, books ever.

Elizabeth Goudge—especially *The Little White Horse.*

China Court, by Rumer Godden.

A.A.Milne's children's books plus *Once On A Time* and *The Ivory Door.*

In self-defense, let me remind you that the list of books is of those reread more than twice. I've almost finished Proust for the second time but I will probably never read it again. And yes, I do read I.A. but rereading would make it hard to keep up with the output. And, as is obvious, I write mostly children's books.

Both Isaac and I hope that the readers of this book have their own personal lists of beloved, reread, and function-ally necessary books. We wish we could see and use all of your lists, but life is short and word processors have a way of looking hungry. . . .

Index

Index